Dying Death and Disposal

Dying Death and Disposal

EDITED BY

GILBERT COPE

LONDON

S·P·C·K

1970

First published in 1970
by S.P.C.K.
Holy Trinity Church
Marylebone Road
London N.W.1

Printed in Great Britain by
The Camelot Press Ltd, London and Southampton

ACKNOWLEDGEMENTS

Thanks are due to the following for permission to quote
from copyright sources:

The Editor of *Concilium*: extracts from an article by Heinrich
Rennings, "Death and Burial; Theology and Liturgy",
and from an article by Theodore Stone and Anselm Cunningham, "The Chicago Experimental Funeral Rite".

Penguin Books Ltd: *The Outsider*, by Albert Camus; *Dying*,
by J. Hinton.

Laurence Pollinger Ltd, the Estate of the late Mrs Frieda
Lawrence, and The Viking Press, Inc.: an extract from
"The Ship of Death", in *The Complete Poems of D. H.
Lawrence*, Vol. II, edited by Vivian de Sola Pinto and F.
Warren Roberts © 1933 by Frieda Lawrence.

SBN 281 02353 0

CONTENTS

CONTRIBUTORS

Charles Brown, F.R.I.B.A., DIP.L.A.
Architect in private practice.

Peter B. Bond, A.A.DIP., A.R.I.B.A.
Architect in private practice.

Gilbert Cope, M.SC., PH.D., DIP. THEOL.
Deputy Director, Institute for the Study of Worship and Religious Architecture, University of Birmingham.

W. Jardine Grisbrooke, M.A., B.D.
Research Fellow, Institute for the Study of Worship and Religious Architecture, University of Birmingham.

John Hick, M.A., PH.D., D.PHIL.
H. G. Wood Professor of Theology, University of Birmingham.

James Mathers, M.B., CH.B., D.P.M.
Medical Superintendent, Rubery Hill Hospital, Birmingham.

Geoffrey Rowell, M.A., PH.D.
Assistant Chaplain and Hastings Rashdall Student, New College, Oxford.

Leonard Tyler, M.A.
Principal, William Temple College, Rugby.

EDITOR: Gilbert Cope

PREFACE

The essays contained in this book are, for the most part, papers which were read at a conference held in March 1968. The conference, entitled *The Last Enemy* (sponsored jointly by the Institute for the Study of Worship and Religious Architecture and the Department of Extramural Studies in the University of Birmingham), was intended to bring into conjunction the many aspects of "Dying, Death, and Disposal" which are usually considered in isolation from one another.

Probably for the first time, therefore, it was possible for an all-round discussion to bring into some kind of relationship those aspects of academic theology, comparative religion, pastoralia, psychiatry, sociology, liturgy, and architecture which are relevant to the successive human situations of terminal illness, committal, and bereavement.

It is unfortunate that two of the original contributions are not available for publication in this volume. However, much of what Professor Ninian Smart said may now be studied in *Man's Concern for Death* (ed. Arnold Toynbee, 1968); further, some reference is made in the Introduction (below) to several important points made in Professor Richard Hoggart's contribution to the conference. To compensate in part for these omissions there is now included a most appropriate background study made by a member of the conference, Dr Geoffrey Rowell, though this was not read at the time.

The conference was attended by a widely representative group of clergy, architects, students, funeral directors, and cemetery superintendents, and the publication of this collection of papers is intended to stimulate further the many-sided debate concerning the problems—theoretical, emotional, and material—which arise from the facts of death.

G. C.

Introduction[*]

Gilbert Cope

The dying, the dead, and the bereaved all need a ministry. Someone has to give help at every stage—a medical ministry, a funeral ministry, and a ministry of comfort. And this is true for every kind of religious believer and non-believer—not least the great mass of Christian half-believers or residual believers.

And, in this many-sided ministry, what is the role of the Church? This itself is becoming increasingly difficult to define, because in the modern urban situation the clergy have "abdicated" from their former position of over-all responsibility: most of their traditional ministry has been taken over and divided up amongst doctors, nurses, psychiatrists, funeral directors, cemetery superintendents, architects, and local authority engineers. It is no exaggeration to say that the role of the clergy is a reduced domiciliary visitation and minimal liturgical recitation.

Much more fundamental, of course, are questions concerning the content and the conviction of what Christians (especially clergy) say to the dying and the bereaved—both personally and liturgically. Death is the ultimate challenge to theology and belief and, in a faith-losing age, these questions have become acutely embarrassing.

All religions are concerned in one way or another to deal with the problems of birth, suffering, and death, and common to most is a theory of spiritual survival—some variant of resurrection or

* The "skeleton" of this Introduction was published in *New Christian* (25 January 1968) partly as a prelude to the conference referred to in the Preface. It has now been rewritten to include additional points made in the discussions during the course of the conference.

1

immortality. Christianity is no exception. And, though the view
that the virgin conception of Jesus is no more than an early christo-
logical myth is generally held not to invalidate the doctrine of an
"incarnation", the consequences of completely de-mythologizing
the New Testament accounts of resurrections would be theologically catastrophic.

In particular, the narratives of the resurrection of Jesus and the
various testimonies to experiences of the presence of the Risen
Lord constitute an irreplaceable heart in the Christian religion.
How are they to be understood today? Is there a modern theologically acceptable alternative to the traditional view? Is there a
corpus of belief called "Christianity" which can survive such
radical restatement and yet remain recognizably the same in
essence?

It is with these problems that Professor Hick wrestles in his
formidable contribution to the academic debate *within* the Church.
But a Christian ministry is not limited to regular churchgoers nor
even to residual or peripheral believers—convinced Christians
also believe that their "mission" should include some elements of
the ministry needed by positive disbelievers in the conditions of
dying and bereavement. The circumstances of death often include
mourners who are agnostic or atheist in their attitudes, and it is
at these points of contact—the bedside and the chapel—that the
challenge is most searching. What does the minister say then about
death and immortality to the humanists in their sorrow? How
does he translate his theology into existentially meaningful
language of comfort?

At the conference Professor Richard Hoggart made a number
of important points which are relevant in any attempt to answer
questions such as these. He discussed the ways in which today's
attitudes to both religion and death have changed: many young
people "just don't think about religion", and death has become
so much a mass phenomenon that it has lost the individual
significance it used to have—especially in the recent past (e.g. the
characteristic death-bed scene of the Victorian novel is unthink-
able in the post-World War II potentiality of mass slaughter).
Further, since the "extended family" (typical of nineteenth- and
early twentieth-century working-class housing and characterized
by a high proportion of deaths in infancy and childhood) has
given way to smaller mobile "nuclear families", funerals have lost

much of their significance as communal acts which "supported" the bereaved in the shock of death and helped to avoid the perils of neurosis. In other words, the "nearness" of death is less familiar, personal, and individual, and is becoming more impersonal and international.

The danger inherent in such tendencies is that it becomes increasingly difficult to pay adequate tribute to the fundamental dignity of the individual person. In the rather elaborate funeral customs of working-class England of a generation ago Professor Hoggart saw above all a desire to realize the proper "respect" due to any man or woman simply because of their status as human beings. The almost "cultic" customs (a lifetime of insurance, prepared shrouds, drawn blinds, raised caps, expensive coffins, floral extravagance, sentimental verse, ham teas, elaborate head-stones) were the sincere attempts of an ill-educated but deeply sensitive people to accord to one of their fellows the dignity which may well have passed unrecognized in his or her workaday life. Such recognition was also that of a community, and the all-too-frequent funerals helped to establish the solidarity of a significant social group pitifully subject to industrial fatality and the ravages of tuberculosis.

Professor Hoggart also insisted that most of the phrases used in connection with death reflected a realistic and stoical acceptance of the stark facts, rather than an attempt to escape from them: there is a literal dignity in "he drew his last breath", and even such euphemisms as "at peace now" and "blessed release" do not necessarily indicate any flight from reality. There is here, of course, a matter for discussion, and current American terminology would seem to reveal a very great reluctance to accept the termination of life and the disintegration of the corpse. Even in England "dead" is recognized as a four-letter word and is avoided by saying that friends have "fallen asleep", "passed away", or "departed".

The psychological difficulty of contemplating one's own non-existence, together with the associated hope of a "waking up", a "return", or an "arrival", leads to the avoidance of the finality implied in the word "dead". Also associated with these attitudes are, of course, a number of other emotions—the distress of bereavement (before and after a death), the fear of suffering and of the unknown—and sometimes a repressed desire to kill.

Yet, even within the past year or so, a new trend is perceptible. More and more books and newspaper articles are being published about death, e.g. two successive issues of the *Observer Colour Supplement*[1] a whole number of *Concilium*,[2] and an essay "The Meaning of Death" by F. A. E. Crew in *The Humanist Outlook*.[3] The latter is a remarkably detached autobiographical account of a distinguished biologist's attitude to his own imminent death and his complete acceptance of the certain (as he believes) total cessation of personality: indeed, he goes further in justifying self-destruction in the event of chronic infirmity in old age. He rejects religion in the following terms:

> The god-hypothesis, invented by man to provide an explanation of the meaning of existence, has served its purpose and is destined to disappear. The old-established religious faiths, in general, are failing to control human thought and action. The decline of Christian theology in the Western World has left a void and since most people need something above and beyond themselves, some ideal, some cause, to which to attach their loyalty and since there can be no return to the simple faith of their forefathers, some new and alternative philosophy must be found.
>
> For my part I find complete satisfaction in the thought that man has taken charge of his own further evolution and also the further evolution of this planet. Than this there could not possibly be a greater adventure, one that must tax to the utmost all the resources that man can muster, knowledge, reason, imagination, aspiration, hope, faith, and a love of mankind.

Such sincere and forcibly expressed testimony is not lightly to be dismissed and those who share this point of view are undoubtedly increasing in number. This is the essence of the humanist challenge to the traditional Christian theology and liturgiology of death and requires an answer which goes beyond devout re-affirmation of former formulations of belief.

The Christian view of death and immortality is now also challenged more immediately by the beliefs and funeral customs of other faiths as these are practised by immigrants to Britain. Not only is there a need to restate the Christian doctrinal position in this situation of confrontation, but Hindu, Buddhist, Islamic, and other burial rites add further complications to the problems of

[1] 27 October and 3 November 1968.   [2] Vol. 2, No. 4, February 1968.
[3] Ed. A. J. Ayer, Pemberton 1968.

cemetery management and crematorium design. (The basic facts are well summarized in the issue of *Concilium* mentioned above— a special number entitled "Death and Burial: Theology and Liturgy").

But, quite apart from what theologians may think and dare to say about death, people will go on dying. A Christian minister has not only to prepare for his own demise, but he has also a pastoral concern for the dying and for the bereaved. Although medical science can do much to alleviate the distress of dying and separation, there remain serious questions of preparing individuals and families for the inevitable and of caring for them in the process. Because there is considerable difference of opinion concerning the most appropriate advice and action in such difficult circumstances, the need for further discussion and exchange of experience is as obvious as is the need for the continued dialogue between doctors and clergy.

The essays of Canon Tyler and Dr Mathers comprise a contribution to this dialogue, and underlying each essay is a great deal of practical experience.

It should, perhaps, be noted that in this volume there is no attempt to contribute substantially to the current debate concerning the "moment of death". This discussion has, of course, been occasioned by recent improvements in the techniques of vital organ transplantation or replacement by "machines". Significant though these developments are in their personal and social implications, they do not appear to raise any *new* religious problems. They certainly complicate some of the existing problems raised by sophisticated medication, but concern to identify or define the "moment of death" would seem to be mainly a matter of forensic medicine. Death is seldom instantaneous, and doctors and lawyers must try to agree on a formula which takes into account the total medico-legal situation. Such a definition is bound to be arbitrary to some extent, and therefore it is most important that it should be both intelligible and generally acceptable to the public. For an excellent discussion of the whole question, readers are referred to A. Keith Mant's well-documented essay "The Medical Definition of Death" in *Man's Concern with Death*.[1]

And then after death—the funeral! What normally happens is a

[1] Ed. Arnold Toynbee, pp. 13–24.

clear reflection of our manifold confusion—both intellectual and emotional. It is probable that most funerary rites and disposal ceremonies are equally distasteful to believers, non-believers, and "don't knows".

First, there is the problem of the liturgy of commendation and committal. Is it possible to devise a rite which is theologically honest and yet does not give offence to conventional Christians in their grief? Is the language of poetry and the imagery of myth justifiable when reason and hope falter? What are we to think about prayers for the dead and the meaning of heaven and hell—not to mention purgatory and limbo? How best may the obsequies be ordered to be an effective part of the ministry to the bereaved?

To these problems Mr Jardine Grisbrooke brings a wealth of learning and a number of provocative suggestions.

Second, there is the whole question of the environment of disposal—cosmetized and enshrouded corpse; coffin in church or undertaker's "chapel of repose"; open earth grave with plastic grass; crematorium chapel with pseudo-altar, badly canned music, sliding doors, or false-bottomed catafalque; gothic chimney-stack, urn-accommodating "columbarium", and "garden of rest". Genuine religious sentiment seems to have been unthinkingly vulgarized and transformed into disagreeable sentimentality.

Admittedly there are very real practical problems to be solved, but it seems that all power of controlling and directing the process and its furnishing (in the broadest sense) has passed from the Church to municipal authorities, private societies, and commercial enterprises. What part, if any, do representatives of local churches have in preparing the architect's brief for a new crematorium? How may current beliefs about death be expressed symbolically in the external location and appearance of the building and its interior furniture and décor? What should be the relationship between the chapel and the incinerator-room?

Further questions may be asked about the psychological effects upon the mourners of the somewhat mysterious disappearance of the coffin and the uncertainty of "what happens next" to the "departed". These and other related questions are discussed very fully in essays by Mr Bond, Mr Brown, and myself.

In the course of the discussions at the conference there was a constant return to a distinction which may properly be drawn between what the bereaved really *need* and what they say they *want*

—between what is psychologically necessary and what is offered by clergy, doctors, and undertakers. Fundamentally the funerary ministry is to the bereaved rather than to the deceased. Neither the decomposing corpse in the earth nor the ground ashes from the crematorium has any theological significance, but it does not follow that the mortal remains should be unceremoniously disposed of as rapidly as possible. On the contrary, the probability is that the ceremonies of death (religious or otherwise) have a considerable therapeutic effect and, therefore, need to be taken very seriously.

Incidentally, the disagreeable trade papers of "morticians" in the United States reveal that they are beginning to get worried because their younger customers now tend to say in effect: "You already do practically everything—why not just take it away and don't bother us any more with the corpse?—just send the bill". By building up such a monstrous business on the basis of sentimental display and commercial vulgarity, they have (so to speak) dug their own graves. A better understanding of the human condition would seek to base the funerary ministry in personal dignity, in psychological understanding, and in spiritual perception rather than in such false compensations for the harsh realities of death in a socially competitive society.

Finally, it is worth recording that the preparations for the conference which provided the papers for this book were often accompanied by uneasy laughter; it has been very noticeable how conversation about dying, death, and disposal generates macabre humour—both unintentional and intentional. Perhaps this is a good sign, for I am convinced that it is possible (and desirable) to be serious without being solemn. We may rejoice that not all the euphemisms for dying are pious circumlocutions and regret that so little in the Scriptures corresponds to our current sense of humour.

1

Towards a
Christian Theology of Death

John Hick

In order that we may start from where we are, and may be reminded of where this is by contrast with somewhere else, let me begin by reading to you two passages from the world we have lost —the world in which the belief in a life to come was a pervasive factor in most people's minds, affecting their attitudes both to life and to death. The first passage comes from a book of legal precedents published in London in 1592, when the first Elizabeth was on the throne of England and when Will Shakespeare was a rising London playwright. The book offers "a verie perfect form of a Will", which begins as follows:

In the name of God, Amen. The twenty-sixth day of April in the year of our Lord God, one thousand five hundred and ninety two, A.B.C. the unprofitable servant of God, weak in body, but strong in mind, do willingly and with a free heart render and give again into the hands of my Lord God and Creator, my spirit, which he of his fatherly goodness gave unto me, when he first fashioned me in my mother's womb, making me a living creature, nothing doubting that for his infinite mercies, set forth in the precious blood of his dearly beloved son Jesus Christ our alone saviour and redeemer, he will receive my soul into his glory, and place it in the company of the heavenly angels and blessed saints. And as concerning my body even with a good will and free heart I give over, commending it to the earth whereof it came, nothing doubting but according to the article of my faith, at the great day of general resurrection when we shall all appear before the judgment seat of Christ, I shall receive the same again by the mighty power of God, wherewith he is able to subdue all things to himself, not a corruptible, mortal, weak and vile body, as it is now, but an uncorruptible, immortal, strong, and perfect body in all points like unto the glorious body of my Lord and Saviour Jesus Christ . . .

and then the testator proceeds to the disposition of his property.

Now this is of course a consciously correct form of words according to the ideas of the time, offered as a paradigm for the framing of wills; and we may perhaps be tempted to wonder if it is more correct than sincere. But I think that any such suspicion would be uncalled for. These words reflect the real beliefs of real people.

As indirect evidence of this I cite a second passage. This was written nearly 200 years later, and is to be found in Boswell's *Life of Johnson*, where he transcribes a page of Johnson's diary for Sunday, 18 October 1767.

Yesterday, Oct. 17, at about ten in the morning, I took my leave for ever of my dear old friend, Catherine Chambers, who came to live with my mother about 1724, and has been but little parted from us since. She is now fifty-eight years old.

I desired all to withdraw, then told her that we were to part for ever; that as Christians, we should part with prayer; and that I would, if she was willing, say a short prayer beside her. She expressed great desire to hear me; and held up her poor hands, as she lay in bed, with great fervour, while I prayed, kneeling by her, nearly in the following words:

"Almighty and most merciful Father, whose loving kindness is over all thy works, behold, visit, and relieve this thy servant, who is grieved with sickness. Grant that the sense of her weakness may add strength to her faith, and seriousness to her repentance. And grant that by the help of thy Holy Spirit, after the pains and labours of this short life, we may all obtain everlasting happiness, through Jesus Christ our Lord; for whose sake hear our prayers. Amen."

I then kissed her. She told me, that to part was the greatest pain she had ever felt, and that she hoped we should meet again in a better place. I expressed, with swelled eyes, and great emotion of tenderness the same hopes. We kissed, and parted. I humbly hope to meet again, and to part no more.

Here there is I think no mistaking the genuine and full sincerity of the beliefs that are expressed.

These documents, with their presuppositions, come as I have said (using Peter Laslett's recent title), from the world we have lost. The firm assumption that this life is part of a much larger existence which transcends our earthly span is no longer a part of the thought world of today. Post-Christian secular man believes only in what he experiences, plus that which the accredited sciences reveal to him. The afterlife falls outside this sphere and is accordingly dismissed as a fantasy of wishful thinking. Of course not everyone you meet in the streets is an example of post-Christian secular man come of age, as depicted after Bonhoeffer. On the contrary, many different phases of pre-Christian, Christian, and post-Christian existence coexist in our culture and even sometimes within the same individual. There may even in our society as a whole be more pre-Christianity than post-Christianity, with more people believing in astrology than astronomy, or putting their faith in horoscopes rather than in microscopes as means to knowledge. So far as afterlife beliefs are concerned, a B.B.C. report of 1955 suggested that about 43% of its public (which is virtually coterminous with the population as a whole) believes in a life after death. If such is the nation-wide state of mind on the subject, there is good evidence that this has influenced opinion within the churches, drawing it down towards this half-hearted (or to be more precise 43%-hearted) level of belief. For example the Mass Observation document *Puzzled People*, published in 1948, reported that "Of those who say they believe in a Deity, one in five are definite in their assertion that they do not believe in a life after death." And in the Gallup Poll's *Television and Religion* survey, published in 1964, it emerged that some 74% of Roman Catholics in this country believe in an afterlife, some 56% of Free Churchmen, and some 49% of Anglicans. These figures are for the official or nominal memberships. The figures for regular church attenders are higher and are grouped closer together, namely Roman Catholics 88%, Free Churchmen 86%, and Anglicans 85%. But that there are 12–15% of regular committed worshippers who do not believe in a life after death is surely significant, and indicates a fairly marked movement away from traditional Christian teaching on the matter. And this negative attitude, which may for some 15% of church members be simply an assumption absorbed from the surrounding culture, has been turned by some of our more radical theologians into a principle for the reinterpretation of Christianity. Authentic Christianity, they say, has no place for afterlife beliefs. Christians are not and ought not to be interested in the possibility of an existence after death. We ought instead to be wholly interested in this world and in our contemporary neighbours, with their and our pressing human needs and problems.

In commenting upon this point of view may I begin by indicating my personal starting point?

In general I have far more sympathy with the new theologians than with the old theologians. I regard the contemporary breaking of long-established religious thought forms as good, and as having inaugurated a period in which there are exciting possibilities of reconstruction and challenging scope for originality. Thus in face of the contemporary theological ferment I do not, when I try to look into my own mind, feel reactionary, censorious, or defensive. I have even, when I was in the United States, been involved in a heresy case, when a very conservative minority sought to exclude me from the ministry of the United Presbyterian Church for declining to affirm one of the more manifestly mythological aspects of the Christian tradition. I mention this simply to indicate that if I now proceed to criticize the understanding of death offered by the new theology this criticism does not necessarily come out of a generally reactionary attitude, nor out of a constitutional failure to comprehend or sympathize with the new. But I am nevertheless bothered by a tendency in popular radical theology today to set up false, because over-simple, alternatives, and consequently to arrive at unwarranted conclusions.

It appears to me that in this matter of the afterlife we have a case in point. On the one hand, it seems obviously true that we should not so set our thoughts upon a life to come as to undervalue or fail to engage unreservedly with this present earthly existence. Christianity is concerned with the transformation of human life here and now. Salvation is not something to be postponed to another sphere beyond the grave; eternal life (whatever else it may be) is a quality of living to be entered into now. All this is surely both true and enormously important. But it does not follow or even begin to follow, that there is no life after death. I shall suggest a little later how the two themes of immortality and this-worldliness are fully compatible with one another. But I would simply point out at the moment that the fact that we ought not, in the midst of this life, to distract ourselves by dwelling upon a life to come, does not entail that this earthly existence, upon which we are now meant to be concentrating, is all. The question of a life after death must be decided in some other way.

Unless, then, we choose to regard ourselves as simply the priests of human culture, affirming—only more so—what our culture affirms and denying what it denies, the fact that the public mind of our day is tending away from belief in a life after death does not settle the matter. There remains the possibility that Christianity is committed by its sources and its nature to the claim that the structure of reality is other than that which our contemporary culture as a whole believes it to be. And so we have to raise directly the question whether the belief in an afterlife is or is not an essential part of the Christian faith. Upon this issue every other aspect of our theology of death necessarily hinges.

There are two broad divergent alternatives for Christian thought in relation to each of its main traditional tenets, including eschatology (i.e. its discourse concerning "the last things", one of which is death). In philosophical terms, one of these alternatives is realist and the other reductionist. To outline the latter first: it claims that the meaning of the various Christian doctrines can be wholly stated in terms of present human experience and involves no claim that goes beyond this. The meaning, for example, of the doctrine of creation is that we accept the world as basically good; the doctrine expresses (I quote Paul van Buren) "an affirmative view of the world of men and things".[1] Again, the meaning of the doctrine of the divinity of Christ is that we take him as our Lord. And in the same pattern the meaning of the doctrine of eternal life is our affirmation that the life of faith has unlimited value and significance. There is thus in each case a reduction of—to use a variety of terms—the metaphysical to the psychological, or the ontological to the existential, or the transcendent to the immanent. In contrast to this, theological realism affirms both dimensions and refuses to reduce the one to the other. It does not of course deny that it is part of the meaning of creation that the world is good; or that it is part of the meaning of the divinity of Christ that he is our Lord; or that it is part of the meaning of eternal life that the life of faith has unlimited worth. It is not concerned to say less than this but in each case to say more than this. And so far as eternal life is concerned it claims not only that the life in relation to God has unlimited value but also that this value is

[1] *The Secular Meaning of the Gospel,* p. 177.

embodied in unlimited existence. The ultimately valuable is also the ultimately real. That which God affirms is held in being by his creative love; and accordingly eternal life is also the life everlasting.

There are two main grounds on which this may be affirmed. One is that the teaching of Jesus is so pervaded by the belief in a life after death that it is hardly possible to base one's religious faith upon him, as the revelation of God's love to man, and yet to reject so integral a part of his conception of the divine purpose. I don't think that I need cite a series of New Testament passages to establish that Jesus believed in a future life. I will only mention, by way of reminder, the parables of Dives and Lazarus and of the sheep and the goats; the controversy with the Sadducees about the general resurrection; and the numerous sayings about future judgement. I have in fact never heard of a New Testament scholar who denied that Jesus believed in an afterlife; and the point can probably safely be taken as non-controversial.

If we now go on to ask *why* Jesus believed so firmly in an afterlife, the answer points to the second possible ground for this faith, namely, that it is a corollary of belief in the sovereign heavenly Father. For there would be an intolerable contradiction in affirming on the one hand that God knows, values, and loves each of his human creatures as unique individuals, and invokes in them the desire to realize the highest potentialities of their nature in response to his claim upon them, and yet on the other hand that he has ordained their extinction when they have only just begun to fulfil the divine purpose which has endowed them with those potentialities and aspirations. The divine love and the divine demand alike bestow upon man a dignity transcending that of the beasts that perish. As Martin Luther said, "Anyone with whom God speaks, whether in wrath or in mercy, the same is certainly immortal. The Person of God who speaks, and the Word, show that we are creatures with whom God wills to speak, right into eternity, and in an immortal manner."[1]

Luther is of course here making the large assumption that eternal life must mean, or at least must include in its meaning, the continued existence of distinct individual human personalities after their bodily death. But—let us now ask—is not this a rather crassly literal idea, the sort of thing that today we almost automatically demythologize? May we not think instead, for example,

[1] Quoted by Emil Brunner, *Dogmatics,* II, 69.

of some kind of merging of consciousnesses in a larger whole, a losing of individual personality in something more inclusive, a fulfilment of human existence which does not involve the perpetuation of separate strands of consciousness? Here one time-honoured picture is that of the drop returning to the ocean from which it was temporally separated.

Needless to say, we *can* think in such terms as these; but the question is whether they will satisfy the exigencies of Christian faith which led us to speak of eternal life in the first place. If we affirm the life to come because of Jesus' teaching, it seems that we shall find ourselves affirming continued individual personal existence. If we affirm it as a corollary of the love of God for his human children, again it would seem that we shall be affirming the continuance of the individual personality. It is indeed hard to see on what specifically Christian ground one would affirm human immortality and yet not affirm it as involving continued personal identity.

But if a conception of eternal life in which human personality is explicitly denied a place fails to satisfy the two interlocking motives of Christian eschatology, may we not fall back upon complete agnosticism concerning the form of the life to come and simply declare that in some unimaginable way God's good purpose for mankind will be fulfilled? Death does not cancel God's love for us; and we must rest in this faith without attempting to picture its implications in quasi-earthly terms. Whether it involves continued separate individuality we do not know and we ought not to care. Sufficient that, whatever its nature, our destiny will be determined by the goodness of God. Such a modest and undogmatic approach can hardly fail to appeal to all of us. And yet I think we can also see that it stands in real danger of meaninglessness. Is it a responsible use of language to speak of eternal life, immortality, the life to come, heaven and hell, and then to add that this language carries no implications whatever regarding the continuation or otherwise of human personality beyond the grave? Are we not evacuating our words of all meaning—whilst however retaining their comforting emotive overtones—if we speak at the grave side of the "sure and certain hope of resurrection to eternal life" and yet add as theologians that this hope is completely neutral as between the deceased's present and future existence and non-existence?

I must confess that this seems to me to come perilously close to double-talk. And yet this kind of language is often heard. Let us consider an actual example, which is to be found in the chapter on "Life after death" in Bishop John Robinson's recent popular book *But That I can't Believe!* (1967). This is a book to which on the whole I respond sympathetically. It seems to me a bold and on the whole a successful attempt to communicate the Christian faith in the language of the *Sunday Mirror*, and this is both a difficult and an important thing to do. But the subject of death and resurrection inevitably stands out as an embarrassment for the "new theologian"; for it confronts him with an unmistakable form of the issue which his whole theology is designed to de-emphasize, the issue of transcendence. On the one hand he does not want absolutely and definitively to deny transcendence, for he is aware that ultimately only this can give religious substance to his faith. But on the other hand, knowing that contemporary post-Christian secular man has no use for the idea of the transcendent, he does not want to rely upon it in communicating the gospel. He finds himself wanting both to affirm it and not to affirm it; hence the air of double-talk that is so liable to pervade his discussion. To turn to our example, we find Robinson saying that in the New Testament eternal life is not a doctrine of survival after bodily death but of "a quality of life—here and now—which death cannot touch. Death is put in its place, as powerless to make any difference" (p. 45). This, he notes, agrees with the contemporary attitude that "Death may be the end. So what?" (p. 45). Accordingly, Robinson concludes that "nothing turns on what happens after death" (p. 46). He is apparently saying in this aspect of his discussion that eternal life is a quality of existence available to mankind now, and that to affirm it as the gift of Christ is compatible with the contemporary secular assumption that death means personal extinction. But then, talking in a different vein, Robinson also says (p. 46):

> As a Christian, I know my life to be grounded in a love which will not let me go. It comes to me as something completely unconditional. If it could really be put an end to by a bus on the way home it would not have the quality I know it to have. From such a love neither cancer nor the H-bomb can separate. Death cannot have the last word. . . . As St Paul says, "If in this life only we have hoped in Christ, we are of all men the most foolish."

Here, if words have any stable meaning, he is saying that eternal life is a relationship to God which is not terminated by bodily death. And, if it is not terminated by bodily death, then presumably it goes on after bodily death. Surely, then, the secular reader will rightly want to know whether Robinson is affirming a life after death or not; and in either case he will want to have the matter stated unambiguously and its consequences explicitly acknowledged. (It is worth adding that this criticism does not apply to Robinson's main book on this subject, *In the End, God* . . .).

It is I think to be noted that the logical relationship between the two views which are found side by side in Robinson's chapter is an asymmetrical relationship. The first excludes the second, but the second does not exclude the positive part of the first. We do not have to choose between the alternatives of eternal life as a present quality of existence and eternal life as immortal existence; still less between an infinitely valuable quality with a brief duration and a relatively valueless quality with unlimited duration. These are not the only possibilities. The more authentically Christian view of the matter, I would suggest, goes beyond this false alternative to the conception of eternal life as unlimited both in value and in duration, the link between the two being forged by the love of God which unqualifiedly affirms and supports this special quality of creaturely existence.

This is perhaps the point at which to identify a red herring which sometimes misleads thought on these matters. It is said—correctly—that the distinctively Christian doctrine is not one of immortality but of resurrection. So far from being naturally immortal, as Plato for example taught, the Bible teaches that man is made out of the dust of the earth and is destined to be dissolved again into that dust. But God by his own will and sovereign power recreates us after death in another sphere of being, bestowing upon us a new life which is not a natural immortality but a free gift of the Creator. From this starting point, which represents in capsule the biblical view, some have inferred that there is no Christian doctrine of immortality and/or of human survival after death. But this does not follow at all. The doctrine of God's resurrecting of the dead is not the opposite of a doctrine of human immortality, but is a form of that doctrine—namely, one in which man's immortality is seen as a divine gift and as dependent upon the will of God. This is quite clearly a doctrine of human survival of bodily death and in that sense of man's immortality.

However, if Christianity is indeed committed to belief in personal survival after death, both by its starting point in the life and teaching of Jesus and by the logic of its faith in the love of God for the finite beings made in his image, there now opens before us a further set of options. For there are two major alternative theological frameworks within which the Christian belief in an afterlife has developed; and these tend to produce two rather different attitudes to death.

The tradition which has for the most part dominated the Western Christian mind until our own time is based upon the great imaginative picture, or myth, of the drama of salvation beginning with the fall of man and ending in the division of humanity into the saved and the damned, segregated in heaven and hell. Man was originally created as a finitely perfect creature, but wickedly misused his freedom to rebel against God; and it was this original sin that, in Milton's words, "brought death into the world, and all our woe". Death is thus a punishment for, or a divinely ordained consequence or fruit of, sin—a consequence brought upon the whole race by the sin of our first forefather, Adam. St Paul wrote that "sin came into the world through one man and death through sin, and so death spread to all men".[1] But it was St Augustine in the fifth century who, elaborating Paul's thought in his own way, definitively projected the picture that has informed the Christian imagination for 1,500 years. In the *City of God* he said that "the first men were so created, that if they had not sinned, they would not have experienced any kind of death; but that, having become sinners, they were so punished with death, that whatsoever sprang from their stock should also be punished with the same death".[2]

On this view our mortality is not an aspect of the divinely intended human situation, but is an evil, a state that ought never to have come about, a disastrous consequence of man's turning away from his Maker. Death is a punishment, and the emotions that appropriately reverberate around it are those of guilt and sorrow, remorse and fear.

But the Christian mind has never adhered consistently and

[1] Rom. 5. 12.   [2] Book 13, chap. 3.

exclusively to this understanding of mortality and to the attitude
which it renders appropriate. In addition to this dark, punitive
conception of the meaning of death there has always been the very
different picture of human life as a pilgrimage, with bodily death
as the end of one stage of that pilgrimage and, by the same token,
as a passing on to another stage. This picture has in it a glint of
gold, a note of fulfilment, of triumph, even of adventure in face of
death, a note which is perfectly caught in John Bunyan's passage
about the passing of that great pilgrim, Mr Valiant-for-truth:

> After this it was noised abroad that Mr Valiant-for-truth was taken
> with a summons by the same post as the other, and had this for a
> token that the summons was true, that his pitcher was broken at the
> fountain. When he understood it, he called for his friends, and told
> them of it. Then said he, I am going to my fathers, and tho' with
> great difficulty I am got hither, yet now I do not repent me of all the
> trouble I have been at to arrive where I am. My sword I give to him
> that shall succeed me in my pilgrimage, and my courage and skill to
> him that can get it. My marks and scars I carry with me, to be a
> witness for me that I have fought his battles who now will be my
> rewarder. When the day that he must go hence was come, many
> accompanied him to the riverside, into which as he went he said,
> Death, where is thy sting? And as he went down deeper he said,
> Grave, where is thy victory? So he passed over, and all the trumpets
> sounded for him on the other side.

This pilgrim attitude to death is only at home within a different
theological framework from the official Augustinian understanding of our mortality as a divinely inflicted punishment for sin.
This different framework is to be found within the history of
Christian thinking, though for most of the time only as a minority
report overshadowed by the dominant Augustinian tradition. The
alternative goes back through strands of Eastern Christianity to
the early Hellenistic Fathers, and has been developed more fully
in the modern period since it reappeared in the work of the great
nineteenth-century German Protestant thinker, Friedrich Schleier-
macher. On this view man was not created in a finitely perfect
state from which he then fell, but was initially brought into being
as an immature creature who was only at the beginning of a long
process of moral growth and development. Man did not fall
disastrously from a better state into one of sin and guilt, with
death as its punishment, but rather he is still in process of being

created. Irenaeus, in the second century, provided a vocabulary for this teleological conception when he distinguished between the image (*imago*) and the likeness (*similitudo*) of God in man. Man as he has emerged from the slow evolution of the forms of life exists as a rational and personal creature in the image of God. But he is still only the raw material for a further stage of the creative process by which this intelligent animal is being brought through his own free responses to his environment to that perfection of his nature which is his finite likeness to God.

From this point of view the wide gap, marked by the doctrine of the fall, between man's actual state and the state intended for him in God's purpose, is indeed a reality. But the ideal state, representing the fulfilment of God's intention for man, is not a lost reality, forfeited long ago in "the vast backward and abysm of time", but something lying before us as a state to be attained in the distant future. And our present mortal embodied earthly life is not a penal condition, but a time of soul-making in which we may freely respond to God's purpose and become, in St Paul's phrases, "children of God" and "heirs of eternal life". For such a theology the proper function of our earthly existence, with its baffling mixture of good and evil, is to be an environment in which moral choices and spiritual responses are called for, and in which men and women are being formed in relationship to one another within a common world.

This theology prompts an understanding of the meaning of life as a divinely intended opportunity, given to us both individually and as a race, to grow towards the realization of the potentialities of our own nature and so to become fully human. Life is thus aptly imaged in terms of the ancient picture of an arduous journey towards the life of the Celestial City. This pilgrimage crosses the frontier of death; for its final end is not attained in this life, and therefore if it is to be attained at all there must be a further life, or lives, beyond bodily death in which God's purpose continues to hold us in being in environments related to that purpose.

Accordingly death does not have the absolute significance that it has in the Augustinian theology as the moment when the individual's eternal destiny is irrevocably decided. In that tradition the soul as it is at the moment of bodily death faces a definitive divine judgement and receives either the gracious gift of eternal life or the just wages of eternal death. But this traditional picture has to be criticized in the light of modern biological, psychological, and sociological knowledge. The conditions of a person's life as these are determined by his biological inheritance, and by the influence of the family and the wider social matrix upon his early development, are often such as to make it virtually impossible that God's purpose for the individual will be fulfilled in this life. It would thus be intolerably unjust for such a victim of adverse circumstances to be eternally penalized. From the Christian premise of the goodness and love of God we must accordingly infer continued human life beyond death leading eventually to the far-distant fulfilment of the purpose for which we exist.

Within such a theological framework the question has to be encountered, why is there any such thing as death? If we die only to live again beyond death, why should we die at all? What can be the function of death within the divine purpose, as this kind of theology conceives of it?

I think that some of the things that existentialist writers have said about death point in the direction of an answer by stressing the way in which our mortality determines the shape and character of our lives. This is, I think, an important insight, to which I shall return presently. But before coming to that there is another related suggestion to be considered. It is sometimes said that a man's death gives *meaning* to his life. This is in fact said in two senses, each of which is worth looking at.

First, there is a sense in which a man's death, by completing his life, makes it possible for others to see its meaning. For only when a life has been rounded off by death are we able to see it in its totality and so to characterize it as a whole. And to be able to characterize it as a whole as a good life, or bad, as happy or unhappy, heroic or banal, creative or wasted, and so on, might be equated with seeing its nature and quality, or discerning its meaning. This seems to be true enough; but so far it supplies only a relatively trivial sense in which death gives meaning to life. It applies the general truth that you can only see a process in its totality once it has been completed; from which tautology it follows that one can only see a man's life as a totality after he has died. But nevertheless a life may *have* a meaning—a value, a direction, a purpose—whilst it is still being lived, even though it is only at death that the accounts can finally be closed and audited.

Bertrand Russell, for example, is now ninety-seven years old and has already left much more than an average life-span of activity and writing to be surveyed, evaluated, praised, criticized. We do not have to wait until he dies to be able to see in his life a remarkable living out of the rationalist spirit. We can see his relentless intellectual honesty; the narrowness of some of his thinking as well as the extreme clarity of all of it; the shape of his life as fulfilling Plato's ideal of the philosophic life, which begins by attending to mathematics and logic and ends in engagement with the concrete human problems of ethics and politics. And so massive and consistent has been the quality of his life over this long period that nothing he might do or fail to do now would undo the meaning of the life he has already lived. We are thus reminded that the tautology that we can see a life as a whole, and see the meaning of that whole, only when the life has terminated, is in some cases merely trivial and unilluminating.

But there is a second sense in which a man's death may give meaning to his life, namely that the manner of his dying may throw a flood of retrospective light upon his character throughout life. The analogy has been used of the final resolving chord of a melody: only when this last chord is heard does the melody as a whole emerge. The last act, the act of dying, instead of being just one more event in a man's biography, may constitute a peculiarly crucial and illuminating climax. For example, one who had seemed through lack of severe temptation to be a person of integrity may die ignominiously trying to save himself at the expense of a number of others, and this selfish end then colours our appreciation of his character and of his life as a whole. Or on the other hand an apparently very ordinary man, living an inconspicuously decent and honest life, may in some great crisis sacrifice his life to save others; and then this death reveals to us a quality that was implicit in his life as a whole. He was all that time a man capable of heroic self-sacrifice, though until this last crisis that quality showed itself only in the quiet integrity of his life. Now, however, there is a final burst of illumination in the light of which that integrity takes on a stronger and more dramatic colour.

In parenthesis let me say that by analogy this may suggest a way of understanding the significance, for Christianity, of the death of Jesus. That is to say, Jesus' death has special significance as revealing the significance of his life and work as a whole. His life was a complex event in which the divine love towards mankind was seen at work on earth in the midst of human history; and the depth of that love was finally and definitively revealed by Jesus' willingness to be crucified rather than deny the saving significance of his own life and teaching. In contrast to the traditional satis- faction and penal-substitutionary atonement theories this means that the significance of Christ's death did not reside in the event itself considered in isolation and as effective *ex opere operato*. Christ's saving work was his ministry as a whole. But within this his passion and death have special significance as revealing the dominant motive and meaning of his life.

There is, then, a sense in which a death may give meaning to a life by illuminating the significance already inherent in it. But such illumination is somewhat exceptional. It occurs only in the case of a death, such as a martyrdom, that is in some special way strik- ing and significant. But most deaths are simply the chronological end of a life, and throw little or no additional light upon the meaning of that life. Or they may be the kind of death that is positively destructive of meaning because it breaks into a life prematurely and yet stands in no organic relation to that life and its quality. It is this that makes the atheistic existentialist Jean- Paul Sartre speak of "the absurd character of death".[1] He notes that death may at any moment violently strike a man down in mid-career by accident or disease, leaving his work unfinished, his relationships unfulfilled, his plans disrupted, his potentialities undeveloped. We are all of us, at least until old age, subject to this possibility. And for Sartre the fact that death as arbitrary destruc- tion may befall anyone vitiates the meaning of life. "Thus," he says, "death is never that which gives life its meaning; it is, on the contrary, that which on principle removes all meaning from life."[2]

Sartre is surely exaggerating—and indeed does not a good deal of existentialist thought consist in precisely this kind of exagger- ation?—when he says that the possibility of premature death renders all life meaningless and absurd. (Does for example the possibility that Bertrand Russell may be run over by a bus in his ninety-eighth year now render his already long life meaningless?) However, just as others have been right in saying that in some cases a man's death discloses the meaning of his life, so also Sartre

---

[1] *Being and Nothingness*, p. 533.   [2] Ibid., p. 539.

is right in saying that in some cases death deprives a life of meaning. Death can have both this meaning-bestowing and this meaning-destroying effect. And what, as it seems to me, Christianity has to say at this point is that neither this meaning nor this meaninglessness are absolute and final. Death is the end of the chapter but not of the book; or better, it is the end of the volume but not of the whole work. This life has its own autonomy and may have its own completeness; and all our present activities have to be related to it and to terminate within it. And yet, according to Christianity, death is nevertheless not extinction. The meaning developed in this life, in so far as it is good, is to be taken forward into a larger pattern of larger value; and the meaningless thread of a life without value is not to be cut but is to be carried forward and eventually woven into the same pattern of larger and indeed unlimited value.

And yet it remains a valid insight that it is the boundaries that give to anything its shape; and there is an important sense in which the boundary of death provides the distinctive shape and character of our human life. Consider as an analogy the contribution which the regularly recurring boundaries of sleep make to the nature of our human experience. Even if we did not need this relapse into unconsciousness after every eighteen hours or so for the sake of physical rest we should still need it in order to divide life up into manageable sections. Continuous consciousness from the cradle to the grave, without regular pauses and partial new beginnings, would be intolerable. The ceaseless bombardment of sense impressions, the unremitting engagement of the self with other people and with the circumstances and problems of our lives, would mount up to an unbearable pressure. But in fact this pressure is relaxed every night by the disengagement of sleep, making it possible to begin afresh in the morning. Of course the new day offers only a relative beginning. The world has continued through the night, and yesterday's problems are still there waiting to be taken up again. But nevertheless the very fact of taking them up again offers the possibility of a varied approach. The new day opens up new possibilities. Time has passed; tension has been relaxed; emotions have calmed; our mind has surveyed its problems again and perhaps come to see them slightly differently. And this continually repeated new beginning plays an important part in forming the structure and quality of our experience.

Now perhaps this effect of sleep in dividing our life into parts which, having their own terminus, have each their own shape and character, suggests an analogous function for death. Perhaps we are not ready for the endless vista of eternal life because our life lacks that quality which would alone make welcome the prospect of a limitless future. But perhaps it is the function of mortality to bracket a space within our immortal existence, making a limited span within which to live. Within this horizon there is the possibility of finite achievements and failures in finite situations, and consequently of the growth and development of character.

This view involves both an attitude to life and an attitude to death. As regards the first, it means that we have a limited vista of life set before us, bounded by an end beyond which we cannot see; and upon this limited scene we have to concentrate all our thoughts and efforts. It is long enough for the greatest human plans and achievements, and yet short enough to give shape and urgency to life. Because time is limited it is precious. Because we do not live in this world for ever we have to get on with whatever we are going to do. Thus the attitude to life that follows from this view is in practice a this-worldly attitude involving a full concentration upon the affairs of the present life. And as regards our view of death, this is now related to the eternal life which consists in being eternally the object of God's love. Against this background, death will still always be faced with a profound awe and apprehension which engulfs our whole consciousness. But Christian faith seeks to match death as the totally unknown with a total trust in the love of God. Of course in fact this trust is usually far from total. It shares the wavering and fluctuating character of the believer's consciousness of God in the midst of his long pilgrimage. And accordingly the facing of death is often an ordeal of doubt and fear when for perfect faith it would have the different character of a great transition, coloured by the sadness of parting but not evoking deep dread or terror. We can only say that in so far as the trust is real and operative it must take the final sting out of death, the sting of ultimate meaninglessness and vacuity, and must thereby deprive the grave of its victory over life. There can be meaning and hope even in the moments prior to dissolution. And in the minds of those who are now left with an irreparable void in their lives there can be, mingled with their grief, the solemn thought of the trumpets that are sounding on the other side, and a sense of the loving sovereignty of God both here and beyond the dark mystery of death.

My suggestion, then, is that Christian thought is still committed to belief in a life after death; that there is no advantage in concealing this either from ourselves or from others; but that the Augustinian type of theology in which death is held to be the wages of sin should be replaced by an Irenaean type of theology which sees our mortality in relation to a positive divine purpose of love; and that ministry to the dying and to the bereaved, and the ceremonies of death and disposal, should so far as possible reflect this theological conception of death.

But, needless to say, I am well aware that every one of these theses is, to say the least, debatable; and I put them before you as material for debate.

2

Ministry
to the Dying

Leonard Tyler

I suspect that few clergy who have had much experience willingly undertake the responsibility of attempting to speak about this particular aspect of ministry. In so far as ministering to dying people admits one to some of the most intimate of all relationships, there is a certain natural reserve about drawing on details of one's own experience. In some ways it is almost a breach of confidence and relationship to make too public some of the deep encounters of death. Furthermore, most of us are by now rightly suspicious of simplified techniques of ministry and critical of hastily made generalizations based on personal experience. Dying, like falling in love, has many variables and, no doubt, as many ways of happening as there are cultures and people. I want to examine from first premises some of the problems as well as the opportunities of ministering to the dying. In a way, I want to try to proceed from the known to the unknown. More sharply than in other aspects of pastoral ministry, the care of the dying relates the natural and the supernatural. However much we may see such ministry as preparing people for a future world, the processes of dying are very much rooted in this life and that is where ministry begins—at least the ministry of a faith which acknowledges an incarnate Lord. There is a sense too in which all ministry is exercised to dying men and although the immediate concern of this essay is with the short-term problems of terminal illness, much of it applies *in extenso* to the theology and teaching related to the whole life span. It is a commonplace today to acknowledge that we live in the midst of a civilization which rarely mentions death. In fact, there is a conspiracy of silence about it; whilst the inhibitions about class and sex have largely gone, those concerned with death remain. The lifetime of most of us here has seen the departure of the last remnants of Victorian attitudes and customs. Both dying and the disposal of the dead have become slicker, more hygienic matters than ever before. But the processes of dying are largely hidden away and, for the most part, only professional medical attendants and the nearest relatives are admitted to the intimacy involved. Nevertheless, perhaps there is more interest than at first appears, as is evidenced by the universal interest displayed in the regular reports from the Vatican during the last days of Pope John XXIII, and in our own country during the last week of Winston Churchill's final illness. News reports with details were eagerly awaited and the public response was such as to indicate that many of the old chords of interest can still be struck. It is also true that the final chapter in most biographies still deals with the last illness of its subject and I am told that many readers start here—rather than at the beginning of the book! If we look a little deeper, we also find that attitudes to death have deeply influenced some modern, creative minds and people like Bonhoeffer, Dag Hammarskjoeld, or Simone Weil produced some of their profoundest thoughts out of background meditations related to death and its meaning.

No attempt to understand a ministry to the dying can ignore that in this century we have increasingly had to live with the problem of large-scale, sudden death. Two World Wars and the fact that in the twentieth century, in Europe alone, more people have been killed on the roads than in all the wars in history; events like Vietnam; the too frequent occurrence of industrial accidents; the rapid increase of sudden coronary deaths, show that the human time scale has been largely changed and we have come to accept what we do not appear to be able to prevent. With such a background, the very question about a Ministry to the Dying can seem a leisurely and privileged concern for the few.

I commend to you the recent Pelican *Dying* by Dr John Hinton. On the frontispiece he gives a quotation from La Rochefoucauld: "Neither the sun nor death can be looked at with a steady eye." I would suggest that the Christian response is an attempt to produce such a "steady eye", based neither on fear nor superstition, but on some of the deepest insights and experience which the human race can gather from every legitimate source whether secular or sacred. It is part of our human condition to be aware of death, but if I am right in my researches I am interested to discover that, whilst many different cultures have developed elaborate burial rites for the disposal of their dead, only the Christian culture has attempted to produce any ministry or ritual for those who are preparing for death. Even though sometimes this has been mechanical and superstitious, it is at least an interesting starting point to recognize that the process of dying is in itself an important part of human experience. I suggest it is a part of human experience hallowed by the Christian tradition, not primarily out of fear either of death itself or the unknown beyond but because the love of the eternal God was revealed through a self-conscious act of dying, and the passion narratives in the gospels make it clear that to the end our Lord retained both dignity and the integrity of his personality until darkness fell. I believe that the aim of our ministry to the dying still is the preservation of human dignity and the wholeness of personality—tasks for which we believe in the end the knowledge of God is indispensable. I dislike the idea of a death-bed repentance, but I can see how the objective of ministry may well be to help a dying man or woman to discover a dignity and integrity they have never known in life. When that happens then God can never be far away. Furthermore, the Christian minister may often have to help non-Christians in their last days. It can be a gross invasion of privacy to expect people to accept our dogma or repeat our pieties, but the discovery of human dignity and wholeness of personality can be unquestionably acceptable to God and man, to Christian and humanist alike.

Today we live in a period of change. We are familiar with the widespread decay of religious faith, but this has not yet been replaced by any other philosophy and Dr Hinton's Pelican, whilst it could not in any sense be accused of theological coat-trailing, at least indicates with great sensitivity the needs of the dying. The deep questions of faith and conviction are not excluded.

Today the experience of dying is largely confined to the adult population. Seventy-five years or so ago child death was infinitely higher, and those who have read Eric Newsome's *Parting of Friends*—which is a study of evangelical and tractarian clerical families in the nineteenth century—will have been reminded, as I was, that in those days even the privileged middle-class families found life infinitely more precarious than we do and frequently had to adjust themselves to the problems of early death. This may well have accounted for much of their religious seriousness and for the mawkish piety and morbidity which was characteristic of their letters and their prayers. Today it is very rare for priests to have much experience of ministering to dying children, but I have frequently noticed that parents who have had to endure such bereavement often retain a perplexed sensitivity which leaves them open to profound religious understanding. We should ask ourselves whether, with the continued decline of the traditional practice of faith, the clergy will continue to have a ministering role to the dying, or can that be replaced by technically expert medical or social work care, following what is already known about the psychic and physical needs of the dying. At the very worst, we could see the development of an American mortuary science extended to the period preceding death: at the best, the selection and training of doctors and social workers to cope positively with the problems of terminal illness. I ask whether such technical efficiency could ever do all that needs to be done. Is there some additional quality such as that shown by some devoted nuns in hospices for the dying? Could the compassion that was shown by Quaker and other religious bodies a few years ago for Indians dying in the Bengal famine be replaced by professional, technical skill which did not in the end share the Christian view of man's value and destiny, or at least some philosophy allied to it?

In so far as man has self-awareness, the problems of dying will continue to raise not only the greatest threat to his security, but also the profoundest questions about his ultimate values. Simone Weil said: "Consent to suffer death when death is there and seen in all its nakedness constitutes the final, sudden wrenching away from what each one calls 'I'." From the Christian point of view or, presumably, from any other, ministration to the dying must address itself to the deepest recesses of the 'I' and so it may well be that words, poetry, music, symbols, and the mysterious things of human relationship, such as holding a hand, can touch the deepest and most treasured instincts. I have frequently recited slowly with dying people the words of some well known hymn

such as "When I survey the wondrous Cross" and my experience
is that words of this kind, which have a meaning beyond logic, can
enter the depths of the self-consciousness of the dying person.
Life is complex and rich, so it may well be that in the process of
dying, when all has been done that medical and psychiatric skill
can do, there are recesses of human need which are only touched
by powers greater than logic and reason.

In considering this aspect of ministry, we begin with the
question "What touches the 'I' today?". The experience of dying
and all the associated emotions throws into stark relief much real
human poverty of the human spirit. The things we rightly value
in life—security, work, money, pleasure, learning—look different
on the death-bed. The realities of love and people remain. I
remember once visiting a deceased publican to see him laid out in
the coffin behind the bar pumps so that the customers might pay
their last respects. There he was complete with waiter's coat and tie
and a folded napkin over his arm bearing the words "What we
want is Watney's": a story which leads readily to reflection on
what moves the "I" today!

We live in a world with great emphasis on youth. Experience
counts for little and age is seen as a regrettable necessity which
appears to begin earlier and earlier. Improvements in general
health and the technical ability of modern medicine to cure what
were previously fatal diseases of youth and middle life, have now
given people a self confidence which enables them to postpone the
ultimate questions of human need and destiny. Before we can
decide how to minister we would need to know with much
greater certainty what passes through men's minds: what notions
of death do people possess? The Christian minister needs to find
out about the situation of those to whom he ministers and must
begin with the prevalent tendencies in philosophy, literature, arts
sociology, and psychiatry. A writer like Camus opens up many
doors of understanding and those who would minister sensitively
to the world today whether in its living or dying, need the insights
of the artist as much as the clarity of the theologian. The scene in
the condemned cell in *The Outsider* between the priest and the atheist
murderer Meursault is prescribed reading for all who would minister
to the dying. [1] In his essay "Summer in Algiers" Camus introduces
us to the kind of milieu we will meet in the later book.

[1] A. Camus, *The Outsider*. Penguin 1961, p. 7.

Men find here throughout all their youth a way of living commensurate with their beauty. After that, decay and oblivion. They've staked all on the body they know that they must lose. In Algiers, for those who are young and alive, everything is their haven and an occasion for excelling—the bay, the sun, the red and white checkerboard of terraces going down to the sea, the flowers and stadiums, the fresh brown bodies. . . . But for those whose youth is past no place exists, no sanctuary to absorb their melancholy.

Farther on he gives a brief account of the ethics of these athletes.

The notion of hell, for instance, is here no more than a silly joke. Such imaginings are only for the very virtuous. And I am convinced that the word virtue is entirely meaningless throughout Algeria. Not that its men are without principles. They have their moral code. We don't "chuck" our mothers, we make our wife respected in the street, we are considerate to the pregnant, we don't attack an enemy two against one, because its "cheap". Whoever doesn't keep these elementary commandments "is not a man" and the business is settled.

There are words whose meaning I have never clearly understood [he continues], such as the word sin. I know enough, however, to see that these men have never sinned against life, for if there is a sin against life, it is not perhaps so much to despair of life, as to hope for another life and to lose sight of the implacable grandeur of this one. These men have not cheated; lords of the Summer at twenty through their joy of living, though deprived of all hope they are gods still. I have seen two die, horrified but silent. It is better so. That is the rude lesson of the Algerian dog-days.[1]

Many clergymen will have had the experience when visiting a sick or dying person of having a near relative say: "Of course, I am not religious but I am very pleased you have come." What does such a statement mean, and can we minister with real relevance unless we have first immersed ourselves in the fears and doubts and hesitations of the age? I suggest we must start from what is known and obvious before we can move with confidence to the specifically Christian insights. In ministering to the dying we must first of all relate not our priestly professionalism but our common humanity. There is a place for our doubts and hesitations as well as our faith and convictions. We must feel as men before we can cope as Christians. We stand as man to man and the basic

[1] Ibid., p. 31.

relationship is of this order long before it has any supernatural significance. In the light of this assertion I would make a number of obvious but important points:

1. The priest comes to minister as an outsider. He is, therefore, emotionally removed from the family fears and tension and is freer to enter into the special conditions of relationship which dying permits. In most cases no one else stands in this detached role to the dying person. The priest occupies the position of the trusted, strong man. He is outside the immediate grief situation and in establishing a relationship with the dying person and his relatives he can become an emotional linchpin.

2. He is clearly not a medical attendant and will not submit the patient to any physical discomfort. He is there to do nothing but encounter him as a person or in what remnants of personality the illness still allows. That is a skill calling for love and patience and exposure.

3. Because of his office, the priest is associated with questions of the quality of living and of moral values in the deepest sense. His very presence frequently raises issues for reflection even in the dullest mind. As in all human relationships the silent unspoken thoughts may be the most important.

4. In our particular society the ministering priest will focus whatever residual religious knowledge the dying person possesses. Ideas of God and faith, goodness and love, contrition and amendment, notions of death and resurrection belong to this area of evoked memory. The skill of ministry is to move with certainty, neither too fast nor too slow. The minister should never presume too much nor assume too little. In the end what really matters is the integrity of the relationship. What damage a rough-handed nurse can do to a patient filling him with fear and dread. There can be an equally rough-handed form of ministry; unnecessary prayers, false heartiness, dogmatic pressures, exploitation of fear, mechanical techniques, the sense of hurry, formalism in prayers. Only the skill which comes from experience and a loving spirit, together with ruthless self-honesty, can provide the ground-bed for this particular part of Christian ministry. The dying man is always in a position of helpless dependence. The priest is frequently tempted in this secular age, which has challenged his

general position in society, to exploit with unscrupulous insensitivity any position in which he still has a clearly defined dominant role.

5. By his office, the priest should be able to establish more quickly than most others a confidential relationship of trust and understanding. This should have no strings attached. Its only objective is to preserve human dignity and the integrity of personality. How can God be discovered and his love known if these conditions are not fulfilled? In this way there is a place for valid Christian ministry even to the non-believer or the adherent of other faiths. Dr Hinton in his Pelican refers to the possibilities of this relationship where in visiting himself he says, "We conversed at length or briefly, dependent on their inclination or strength. Many of them said they were pleased at the chance to talk so freely. Often we came to know each other well. Friendship grew fast in these circumstances and sometimes it seemed difficult to believe we met only a few times." This is a frequent experience of the clergy. It ought to be even more frequently our aim.

6. In our world of immense business and activity, where even the immediate relatives have generally to continue with their daily work, the priest is one of the few people who has time to give to what is frequently the slow process of dying. This in itself is a valued contribution.

So far, you will notice that I have said little that is specifically Christian, but I am convinced that sometimes we are in too big a hurry. Before we can minister in a professional capacity or from the insights of faith, we have the natural ministry of men. This can be reinforced by our Christian compassion and patience, but it is the essential prolegomenon to anything more. We are unlikely to get very far today in any Christian tradition by talking too readily about heaven and hell, purgatory or judgement. These are outworn categories of thought. The insights of love, relationship, and human significance may raise much more deeply in the end the issues for which we stand. We live in a secular age and there can be no dichotomy between the rethinking of theology in the lecture room and the pastoral practices of those who seek to make love real in the totality of human need.

Let us look further at all that is most human in this situation, for whether we are Christians or humanists the acceptance and under-standing of death is a human necessity. Dr Hinton points out that amongst the various groups of people whom he observed, those with deep religious faith and practice, together with those who were ardent and committed humanists, were less afraid and more ready to come to terms. It was the indeterminate believers and doubters in the middle who were most hard to help. Let us look at some of the problems which are common to our humanity:

1. Loneliness. Paul Tillich says in his sermon on loneliness and solitude, "There is the ultimate loneliness of having to die. In the anticipation of our death we remain alone. No communication with others can remedy it, as no other's presence in the actual hour of our dying can conceal the fact that it is our death and our death alone. In the hour of death we are cut off from the whole universe and everything in it. We are deprived of things and beings which made us forget our being alone. Who can endure this loneliness?"

2. The need for love. It has often seemed to me that one of the results of caring for the dying and the justification for ministering to them is that they feel that someone cares. They are supported not just by hygienic efficiency but by the love of other people. How often a priest is told that his visit meant more than that of the attendant medical staff. This constantly surprised me because one seemed to have done so little, and yet it may well be that his visit has been a reassurance of loving attention and human value at a point when an individual needed it most.

3. Many dying people fear the loss of control and self-respect. Physical incontinence and emotional distress can be seen as barriers between them and those around. One of the needs of the ministry is to break down this fear. If one has been able to over-come this barrier by holding a vomit bowl or wiping a patient's brow, deep relationships of confidence and trust can be established. I remember ministering to a young woman whose concern was that as she grew more ill she would lose her appearance and charm. I recall her obvious relief when on asking would I come and see her whatever she looked like I replied that of course I would.

4. Dying is a human act and most people wish to do it with what ever dignity and self-control they can muster. How easy it is to treat the seriously sick as less than human, to convey the impression that they are occupying a much needed bed. Sometimes we forget that they can hear what is being said. The use of drugs in terminal illness is a question which raises many issues of human dignity and responsibility. No doubt it is easy to err on the side of over-drugging, and frequently I have been of the impression that hard-pressed doctors have taken the easiest way out too soon.

5. The sense of a life's work being unfinished is one of the problems which looms large on many death-beds, and it was Tillich who said that the anxiety of meaninglessness is potentially as great as the anxiety of death. We live in a society which has put great stress on the value of what we do. Maybe, even for many who are not themselves Christians, the process of dying can be used to teach the basic lesson that what we are is, in the end, more important. To *be* someone is perhaps more significant than doing.

6. The relationship of the dying person to what is being left is a real concern of ministry. The Prayer Book wisely urges those who are near to death to set their temporal affairs in order and to be reconciled to their fellows. This is still done less often than one might expect. More important than the relationship to material affairs are the relationships within families and between friends. Frequently, care for the dying can involve great ministries of human reconciliation. Whether men are Christian or not, this need seems to be common to the human condition and essential to integrity and personal development.

So far, I have still suggested little that is specifically Christian. I have done this deliberately because I believe we have for too long neglected the basis of our humanity out of which we relate to other people and serve them. Before redemption has meaning, our life together in the mysteries of the created world must be explored. In what I have said so far I have made it a primary object that all ministry should seek to maintain dignity and personality in the dying. This is necessary so that the capacity for giving and receiving of love should be maintained to the end. There is considerable evidence that, where these things are right, God can break in. From his own point of view, Dr Hinton comments,

Many dying show their kindness and become perhaps more noble in spirit than they have ever been. They do all they can to spare the feelings of those they are going to leave behind to bear their loss, before relatives visit they prepare their appearance and compose their faces so that those who love them should not believe they suffer. They demonstrate their affection in both apparent and subtle ways. These are the people who often take great care of the feelings of their nurses and doctors. In candid moments, where they know it is possible to speak freely without embarrassment, these generous souls may tell how they help those around them.

It is in responses like this that the reality of God becomes a possibility. But such situations cannot be forced, they must be gently and patiently nurtured. One of the things learned from ministering to many dying people is that physical, psychic, and spiritual needs are all interrelated. Holding a hand or wiping a brow can be as meaningful as a prayer and, if spontaneous, frequently more helpful. The sheer physical weakness and weariness of dying makes possible a profound sacramental significance in the most ordinary actions. So it would appear that, where those who care for the bodily needs are also sensitive to the spiritual needs, there is the possibility of the most complete ministry.

I am brought now to the observation that we still need to do a considerable amount of research into some aspects of the environment within which ministry to the dying is exercised. The classic discussion has generally been along the lines of the differences between ministering to those who have a definite background of faith and practice and those who lack it. But in the confused religious situation of this age, such distinctions mean very little and, unless the Christian minister is prepared to contract out of his responsibilities to all men and resort to a ministry confined to the small percentage of committed, practising Christians, he will need to ask some fundamental questions. For instance, I have observed four quite distinct categories of terminal care which affect the atmosphere within which the minister has to work, for example:

Cases in which old people are caring for the old.
Cases in which young people are caring for the old.
Cases in which old people are caring for the young.
Cases which are being nursed during their last days in hospitals or institutions.

There are also quite distinct problems when a patient is known to have a fatal illness but in which there are temporary remissions and days on end when most of the normal activities of life can be undertaken. This is frequently known in cases of leukaemia. I suggest that any future study of the problems of ministering to the dying would need to look in detail at the implications of situations of this kind, and no doubt there are others that could be discovered.

One of the recurring features of the process of dying concerns the confusion about the passage of time, and sometimes a dying person has little sense of whether it is night or day and, in spite of frequently asking the time, he obviously lives in a new sort of time sequence. I am not sure what the implications of this are, but it is a frequent observation that often immediately after death a person will look twenty or thirty years younger. It is also a common experience to find old memories of names and incidents recalled in the last stages of terminal illness. Frequently, too, in spite of apparent unconsciousness the patient will respond to the familiar words of a prayer or sometimes try to utter the name of some person who has stood in a special relationship to them. This, too, can sometimes go back over many years and cause surprise to those who are at the bedside. I would like more precise studies to be done in this field. What I am suggesting at this point is that the time cycle of past, present, and future takes on fresh meaning for many people during their final illness.

It is here that I suggest the specifically Christian ministration of Holy Communion has profound meaning, for it is clear that in this simple, sacramental act the human experiences of past, present, and future would seem to converge. The material things of bread and wine focus the past and, to the Christian, the recalling through these symbols of Christ's passion and death is profoundly meaningful. But the act of participation is in the present, on the actual death-bed and in the situation in which people find themselves. It is also an action with profound future anticipation, and the words of administration—praying for the preservation of "body and soul unto everlasting life"—introduce an eschatological element which lifts the mind from the things of the past, through the present, to hopeful anticipation of the future and the consummation of all things in the presence of God. Furthermore, the Eucharist is never an individualistic act, and whether the Last

Sacrament can be shared with friends and relatives, or only with the visiting priest, there are visibly demonstrated truths about our humanity, our membership one with another, and the relationship of the one to the many which tie the mysteries of life together.

I have tried in this paper to set out not final answers but a line of thought. I have tried to avoid the trivialities of technique or the impression that this can ever be an easy form of ministry. In the presence of death we stand before the oldest of human mysteries and I would like to end with a quotation neither from Scripture nor from a priest's handbook, but from a poem by D. H. Lawrence:[1]

> Now it is autumn and the falling fruit
> and the long journey towards oblivion.
>
> The apples falling like great drops of dew
> to bruise themselves an exit from themselves.
>
> And it is time to go, to bid farewell
> to one's own self, and find an exit
> from the fallen self.
>
> Have you built your ship of death, O have you?
> O build your ship of death, for you will need it.
>
> The grim frost is at hand, when the apples will fall
> thick, almost thundrous, on the hardened earth.
>
> And death is on the air like a smell of ashes!
> Ah! can't you smell it?
> And in the bruised body, the frightened soul
> finds itself shrinking, wincing from the cold
> that blows upon it through the orifices.
>
> And can a man his own quietus make
> with a bare bodkin?
> With daggers, bodkins, bullets, man can make
> a bruise or break of exit for his life;
> but is that a quietus, O tell me, is it a quietus?
>
> Surely not so! for how could murder, even self-murder
> ever a quietus make?
>
> O let us talk of quiet that we know,
> that we can know, the deep and lovely quiet
> of a strong heart at peace!

[1] From *The Ship of Death*. Faber and Faber, 1941.

"A strong heart at peace"—that would seem to be a sufficiently noble objective for all Christian ministry whether to the vigorous or to the dying. We tend to be squeamish and reluctant to speak of these things. The Christian faith, though not preoccupied with death, has no excuse to avoid the issue. It is a response to the eternal love of God revealed through him who set his face steadfastly to Jerusalem, finally to cry, "Father into thy hands I commend my spirit." "It is finished." There, if ever, was "a strong heart at peace". So to live and die is to be "in Christ".

3

Ministry
to the Bereaved

James Mathers

Birth and death are the only two experiences which are entirely inescapable for a human being. They occur only once in a lifetime, so each of them presents us with a crisis, a situation which is new to us, which involves a drastic change in our relation to the environment to which we have become accustomed, and the outcome of which we cannot foresee.

The loss of someone we love, bereavement, is another crisis which few of us escape. For most of us it will occur more than once; but, unlike death, we have to go on living after it; and, unlike birth, it is an experience which we are able to talk about with other people. It is only one of a large number of experiences of crisis which mark a man's progression from cradle to grave; and I want first to make some observations about crisis experience in general.

We face a crisis whenever we face a situation or life-problem which previous experience has not taught us how to solve. We perceive it as either a loss of something or some relationship we have depended on heretofore; or the threat of such loss; or as a challenge—to give up something we've depended on in the hope of gaining some greater good. Crisis is characterized by the disturbance of an existing stable relationship to our material and psycho-social environment, and the resultant instability means that we are more easily influenced by our surroundings, for better or worse. Subjectively, we feel upset, and show a rise in emotional tension. Often this tension leaks out in irritable behaviour which seems irrelevant and inappropriate. Sometimes we become obsessively preoccupied with one minor facet of the whole problem confronting us, and seem unable to pay attention to other aspects of it which it would be more profitable to tackle. Our distress makes us likely to behave in ways which may evoke helping responses from other people, like a baby crying, though such behaviour is not always consciously determined or acknowledged.

No organism likes to remain in an unstable state for very long, and throughout the crisis period the whole person—body and mind together—is actively seeking ways of restoring stability, finding a new equilibrium. Optimally, the crisis-problem is solved by a newly-acquired understanding of what the situation needs. In such a case, crisis has been the occasion of learning, the person has achieved a greater maturity; and if the problem situation recurs, the repertory of possible responses is so enlarged that its solution is no longer perceived as a crisis of the same magnitude.

But all too often, the human organism finds the emotional tension rising to an intolerable degree, so that relief of this becomes too urgent to wait upon the understanding which would really solve the problem; and a sub-optimal or pathological "solution" is found which, while easing tension for the time being, only serves to bind the person to his still unsolved problem. Such a sub-optimal solution is usually manifest as a physical or psychological symptom or neurotic character trait, while the person is likely to be more upset, rather than less, by a recurrence of the problem-situation. The cardinal practical point for anyone engaged in a ministry to those in crisis, therefore, is the great importance of enabling the person to face the reality of his situation, rather than allowing or encouraging a way of escape from the tension involved which doesn't help solve the real problem.

Perhaps bereavement is more often a crisis than it ought to be. Although an unexpected death is bound to be a crisis, when death occurs in old age or after a long illness, there has been time for those concerned to get used to the prospect. Mature people will no doubt often have done much of their grieving before the death of the loved one in such a case, and perhaps the dying member of a pair of lovers may be the best comforter for the survivor; but sometimes people aren't mature enough: they can't bear to think of it, and they go on pretending to themselves that it won't happen. When it does, the crisis is the more shattering. However, even the most mature of lovers is likely to find the actual death of the partner critical to some extent, for hope dies hard among those who love; and it is not surprising that there is a high death-rate and sickness-rate in the first year of widowhood.

There are many meanings hidden in our use of the word "love", but there are two which are relevant here: the love of the small child for its mother is largely a passive-dependent affair; while the love of the mother for her infant is a caring, self-giving relationship. Adult love relationships contain elements of both these in varying degrees, and so bereavement is likely to have an ambiguous meaning. Inasmuch as the survivor has been the dependable partner, who could care for the other without thought of self, the loss of the other will be painful and tragic. At his most mature, a man cannot give his heart to another without himself dying a little when the loved one dies. By contrast, inasmuch as the survivor has been dependent on the other, like the child who loses a parent, his feelings will be likely to contain an element of anger at his dereliction, and he will have doubts and fears about how he can survive without the other.

As I say, most love relationships contain elements of both sorts of love, so the experience of bereavement quite often contains feelings of anger against the departed. Because it conflicts with the sadness and resignation which seems more appropriate and is socially acceptable, such anger is often denied direct expression, and finds instead an outlet in projections of blame on to other people. You will often find a grieving person blaming the hospital or the doctor or other relatives who didn't seem to care enough— or even blaming himself—for what happened. This seeking for a scapegoat illustrates the kind of mechanism which the mind uses unconsciously to relieve feelings of tension, but which makes no useful contribution to the solution of the real problem—in this case becoming resigned to the fact of bereavement and seeking new relationships to replace the old.

Denial is another tension-relieving mechanism. It is of course more or less normal in the immediate catastrophic reaction to sudden death: our minds refuse to take it in at first, and we continue to act as if it hadn't happened. But once the immediate crisis period is over, denial can be seen to be increasingly abnormal and inappropriate. Many a bereaved wife has thought she heard her dead husband walking through the door, but only a few persist with hallucinations of this kind for long. However, some will persist, for shorter or longer periods, in keeping their husband's desk or wardrobe exactly as it was when he was alive. I recall a mother whose son had been killed in a motorcycle accident when he was nineteen. He had been dead a year when I visited her; and when I went into her house there on the sofa in the hall were his crash-helmet and motorcycling clothes still spread out ready for him to wear. His room and personal possessions were kept cleaned but unmoved. Such behaviour might be tolerably adaptive for an elderly widow with the house to herself. It was clearly not so for this woman, whose husband was embarrassed and whose thirteen-year-old daughter was emotionally neglected by her mother's concentration on the dead son's memory. This woman's prolonged mourning reaction was marked by considerable anger and resentment, which she directed at his companions on the night of the accident and the hospital which treated his injuries. Her relationship with her son seemed to have a large element of dependence on her part: she had been over-attached to him and felt she "couldn't do without him".

Another way in which people may express the anger which comes from over-dependency on the dead person is to blame God. "I can't go on believing in a god who would allow this to happen." They don't always say "who would allow this to happen *to me*", but this is what they mean. It is only the person who has achieved the maturity of a caring, self-giving relationship to the other, dependable rather than dependent, who can accept the situation with grief but without anger, and say, like Job, "The Lord gave, and the Lord hath taken away. Blessed be the name of the Lord."

Perhaps we can now see some of the principles which should govern our ministry to the bereaved, at least those which have a relevance to preventive psychiatry, and the minimizing of subsequent ill-health. The death of a loved one presents a problem which requires considerable effort and hard work to solve. Because the work of mourning is so arduous, it is a great help to have the moral support of understanding friends at such a time. There are the practical details of daily life to be carried on in a bereaved household, and during the initial stages of numbness and yearning the survivors are not well able to cope with these. People who need to express their grief outwardly should not be discouraged. Tears are a relief, especially when they can be shed in the presence of someone who understands but whose own involvement in the situation is controlled. At suitable moments, the bereaved should be encouraged to talk and reminisce about the dead. Part of the healing process of active resignation lies in recapitulating one's experience of the lost—making a sort of inventory of memories, good and bad; and if the bad memories as well as the good can be outwardly acknowledged and shared the healing will be better. This kind of confession and affirmation of what the dead meant to the living can lead to forgiveness at a time when it may be critical for future mental health: the unforgiven dead can blight the life of the survivor quite as much as the unforgiven living.

Conversely, any tendency for the survivor to evade doing the work of grieving by projection or denial should be gently discouraged by directing attention back to the reality of the loss, perhaps by discussion of some practical problem involved—for instance in the change of role from wife to widow.

The business of caring for the bereaved is not easy. Few of us really enjoy entering a house of mourning. People who have suffered a severe loss are seldom at their most attractive. A gloomy mood is catching, particularly if we expose ourselves to it unthinkingly and without care. So are the tension and irritability which are evoked by the crisis. It is all too easy, and all too common, for well-meaning comforters to aid and abet the sufferer in escaping from the tension rather than facing the problem realistically. We tell him to "snap out of it" or we say "you mustn't brood" or "you must hide your feelings" or "you should take a holiday and get right away for a bit". And the reason we offer this cheap comfort is because we ourselves are unwilling or unable to face the reality of the experience of death and bereavement.

This leads us to realize that it is an essential part of our practical ministry to the bereaved that we should ourselves come to terms with our own fears and doubts about the matter. Some people, who have suffered bereavement in adult life and who have been able to accept such a crisis as a challenge to greater spiritual maturity rather than as a crippling loss, will have learnt the lesson through personal experience. But other people than these may be called upon to minister to the bereaved. How can they come to terms with it?

As a medical student, I was never taught how to help people deal with the fact of death. I suppose this is understandable, even if regrettable. A doctor's job is to help people live a full life, and if he were too constantly aware that death was the inevitable outcome of all his efforts, he might be a less welcome visitor in a sickroom. But people in general, particularly the relatives of those who are sick, tend to take doctors seriously. So if we adopt the attitude that death is at all times something to be fought against, evaded, not even to be thought about or spoken of, then folk will follow our example.

To illustrate: Many doctors still believe that it is unwise ever to tell a patient that he has a disease from which he is likely to die. Not only will they evade telling the patient, which may sometimes be wise, but they will tell the truth to the relatives—and then instruct them to evade telling the patient too. This can cast a shadow over the last few weeks or months of a loving partnership between two who have never had any secrets from each other, and can leave the survivor with a sense of guilt to add to his grief. I don't think a doctor can ever be as good a judge of whether to tell or not as is someone who knows and loves the sufferer.

Five mothers in a maternity ward formed a happy and friendly group in the joy of their new babies. Tragically, one of them died suddenly from a pulmonary embolism. Naturally the others all asked questions about it—how would the baby get on, what would the husband do, and so on. But the nursing staff acting on the doctors' instructions refused to allow any discussion of it. Death was a subject that was taboo.

Such evasions of the reality of death are rather typical of doctors, especially if they work mainly from hospitals. It is an unsatisfactory attitude. All through human history the death of the individual has been recognized and faced up to as a real experience in rituals of burial or burning. A funeral traditionally was a solemn and public occasion, when the members of a community stopped what they were doing and gave themselves time to reflect on the inevitability of death, time to get adjusted to it, time to make real for themselves John Donne's thought that "any man's death diminishes me because I am involved in mankind". It still is in rural districts, but with the coming of the internal combustion engine and the hurry and bustle of the modern city, the tendency is for the funeral to become a private affair for near relatives only. Someone has said that our attitude to death is becoming like the Victorian attitude to sex—it is necessary, but so long as the decencies are observed, the less said about it the better.

Much of our evasion of the subjective reality of death stems from our growing sensitivity to one another's feelings. One would like to think this was truly compassionate but it is often mere sentimentality. In more primitive ages and places it was—and is— impossible to evade the contemplation of death. Few households escaped the experience of having a child die in their midst; war involved face-to-face killing, the destitute died in the streets, executions were performed in public. In former days men were much more aware of the need to make a good death—if only because of the likelihood that it would be a public performance. But in the last few—very few—generations, we have cut down infant mortality, we abolished public executions only a hundred years ago and have hardly done away with capital punishment; while in war we only kill at a distance. Even on the roads our contact with those about to die is through a glass windscreen, darkly, rather than face-to-face.

Perhaps reflection upon our unconscious, absentminded evasions of the thought of death may help us to become more objective and a little less fearful of discussing it with others. It may also help us to contemplate, with intelligent forethought and imaginative sympathy, what our own deaths will mean for those we leave behind, and, conversely, what their deaths will mean for us. Such thoughts do in fact occur to all of us one way or another; but don't we usually tend to keep them private, as if they were somehow indecent? And if they do enter conversation, the embarrassment they raise is dealt with by joking about them—which may be a healthy way of evading the embarrassment, but is an evasion just the same. If my son were to tell me that he had dreamed that I was killed in a car accident it would probably evoke some sardonic remark about wish-fulfilment dreams; but if he were to contemplate the same possibility in full consciousness he would really be showing intelligent anticipation; and would thereby doubtless be better able to cope with the bereavement crisis if and when it occurs.

Now I want to consider the possibility that some of our religious convictions may contain an element of evasion of the reality of death. Some people talk of the afterlife in a way which suggests that they assume a prolongation of time, as we understand it, into infinity. But how do we know that eternity is like this? I suppose that for many of us the essential thing about death is that it is "I", *my* ego, *my* self, or *my* soul, which we are reluctant to part from— that part or aspect of us which seems to endure through time in spite of all the changes and chances of this world. We are all nowadays ready to accept that the next world is not located in space, so we do not worry about our future shape or place. But if the time dimension doesn't exist in eternity either what will a self or soul be then? We can't imagine it. This doesn't of course mean the next world doesn't exist; it only means that I am doubtful if any of us yet understand what our self or soul really is. Since the work of Freud we are slowly beginning to accept the fact that we don't really know ourselves: that most of our lives are governed by impulses of which we are unconscious. We dream, and find our dreams unrecognizable as productions of our own imaginations. Who is the dreamer who dreams my dreams? He is a stranger to me, outside my control. Am I responsible for his thoughts? Is he a part of myself? Am I going to be answerable for him on the day of judgement? Is he going to die with my mortal body, or is he part of my immortal soul?

The relevance of such considerations is that I suspect our anxiety about death and bereavement to be linked with a failure to transcend our egocentricity. Currently, theologians are striving to recover an understanding of the corporate or social aspects of the faith, in the light of modern work in the field of social psychology. We accept that—to quote S. de Diétrich—"God does not call isolated individuals, he creates a community". But we still tend to think of death as an individual affair. To balance this, it may be profitable to contemplate the individual man as a cell in a social organism. We can then consider his death as analogous to the death of a cell in the biological organism. When we talk of the life of a man, we should remember that there is no life in him save that which is manifest in the life of his component cells. And that these cells reproduce, perform their special tasks, and die according to their kind. The brain loses 50,000 cells every day after a man is twenty-five years old, and none of them is replaced. His red blood cells perform no essential function until they are already degenerating, and then they only last four weeks.

Whether we look at the physical organism or at the social organism, the death of the individual component unit is an essential necessity to the continuing life of the whole. In social organisms where there is a high degree of mutual trust and understanding, where morale is high (as in Scott's expedition to the South Pole, or in an army in time of war), the individual does not find it impossible to value the success of the whole body above his own personal survival. Not every soldier who willingly goes forward into danger is exceptionally heroic, or has a firm belief in personal immortality, but his behaviour is admirable because—perhaps in spite of himself—he transcends egocentricity.

The vision of the social organism, however rarely it may be actualized in our own experience, does seem to take us one step away from that egocentricity which gives such a sting to our personal deaths and bereavements. It seems to lead in the direction which St Paul pointed out for us, in his vision of the spiritual organism, the resurrected body of Christ.

In summary then: at the practical level, a ministry to the bereaved should follow the general principles of a ministry to those in crisis. These include material aid and comfort and moral support while the sufferer does his hard work of grieving. The major task, to which the others are subsidiary, is that of enabling the mourner to face the reality of his situation; and, because this reality is something which he has to experience subjectively, the helper has to make an effort of imaginative sympathy; he has to try in some degree to enter into the other's experience while controlling his involvement. This is necessarily a painful process for the helper. To fit himself for it, I have suggested that he should reflect upon the phenomenon of death, and try to discern in advance the ways in which his own mind strives to avoid facing the issues of death and bereavement in his own life; whether by simple refusal to consider it, by a sentimental evasion of the unpleasant tension it arouses, or by fantasies rationalized under the guise of religious belief. Perhaps a full realization of the daily Christian experience of dying to self is the best preparation for helping those who are bereaved.

4

Nineteenth-century
Attitudes and Practices

Geoffrey Rowell

The environment of our cemeteries and the tradition of mourning practices which we have inherited has been deeply marked by the ideas and aspirations of the nineteenth century. That its influence should have been so great is not surprising. It was the first period in which the setting of death was largely urban, with the consequence that the older provision for burial, the churchyards, became inadequate, thus necessitating the opening of large new cemeteries away from any ordinary church building. The older traditions of providing more or less permanent memorials to the departed survived, however, even though the close-knit village communities, in which they had a long-term significance, no longer existed as the background to many deaths. Moreover the death-rate—and particularly the infant mortality rate—remained high until very late in the century. There was also in existence a larger, and increasingly more prosperous, middle class, anxious to ape the aristocratic sepulchral glory of an earlier age: it is not surprising that the new cemeteries quickly became filled with the profusion of marble monuments we know so well.

The nineteenth-century understanding of death was still largely formed by the Christian tradition. The influence of a Calvinist theology had given death a great importance as the moment when the saved testified to their faith and demonstrated their election. In some forms of Evangelicalism the concept of a good death was so developed that there could almost be said to have been a prescribed etiquette for dying. Last words assumed a disproportionate

49

importance, and the cult of the death-bed is reflected in countless Victorian novels. The rise of romanticism certainly contributed to a more general interest in death, sometimes morbid and ghoulish, sometimes more serious, springing from a belief that emotion was revelatory of truth about the human condition. The agonies of bereavement and the suffering of the death-bed thus afforded man an insight into the meaning of life. This interest in death is already present in eighteenth-century works which have links with both romanticism and the Evangelical Revival, such as Edward Young's poem, *Night Thoughts,* and James Hervey's *Meditations among the Tombs,* both of which enjoyed considerable popularity until well into the nineteenth century. Later writers could wax eloquent about the "poetry of death", and a Catholic devotional writer, such as F. W. Faber, could talk of "the grave and pleasant cheer of death".

With such an attitude to death dominant for the greater part of the century it is not surprising that there were numerous discussions of funeral practices and the design of memorials. The most notable campaigners for change in this area were the ecclesiologists, the members of the Cambridge Camden Society. John Mason Neale specifically mentions association with the memorials of death as one of the advantages to be gained from the pursuit of ecclesiology, and this concern with the moral improvement of the living is one which occurs in nearly all advocates of change in funeral practice. The main target of the ecclesiologists' wrath, with their belief in "Gothick" as the only "Christian architecture" and their idealization of the Middle Ages, was the pagan nature of much contemporary funeral practice, and the irreverence which seemed to them to characterize many burials. Neale himself gives the first evidence of his break with a narrow Evangelicalism in a poem he wrote after attending his uncle's funeral at the new Kensal Green cemetery in 1839:

> Take hence the heathen trappings, take hence the Pagan show,
> The misery, the heartlessness, the unbelief of woe;
> The nodding plumes, the painted staves, the mutes in black array,
> That get their hard-won earnings by so much grief per day:
> The steeds and scarves and crowds that gaze with half-suspended breath
> As if, of all things terrible, most terrible was death. . . .[1]

[1] J. M. Neale: MSS. Journal. St Margaret's Convent, East Grinstead.

Neale goes on to plead for a restoration of evidence of a firm belief in the Christian hope in contemporary funerals.

The *Ecclesiologist* published numerous articles on funeral practice. In 1845 it lamented the "atheistical character of funeral processions" and complained of the exorbitant charges of undertakers—ever a favourite point of attack for funeral reformers. The following year there was a further lament:

> Now is the time for the *"Maison de deuil"*, the "Parisian Mourning Rooms", with a "Gothic entrance in Regent Street"; which "are opened to the public for the supply of every description of FASHIONABLE MOURNING IN THE PARISIAN STYLE, of first rate excellence, etc.". Can we go on with patience to mention "the Economic Funeral Company", or Shillebeer's one-horse "hearse-coach", the cold Pagan cemetery, perhaps even the "Necropolis"; the patent cast-iron tressel with its cramps and pulleys . . .? These modern inventions are even worse than the old kind of burials, with their kid gloves, and seed-cake, and feathers, and "the funeral pue".

The "Christian funerals" the *Ecclesiologist* wished to see would be chanted, with no difference in ceremony between rich and poor. Coffins would be straight-sided and gabled with a cross on the top; palls and mourning cloaks would be provided for the poor; coffins would be carried on biers, not on the shoulders, and where a hearse was used it would be in the approved Gothick style with a gabled roof. White would be employed for the funerals of the young and burial clubs with a religious bias would be encouraged.

Robert Brett, a London doctor, perhaps went the farthest towards putting the ecclesiologists' recommendations into practice, with his foundation of the Stoke Newington burial guild in 1856, which became the model for many others. According to his beliefs, a burial guild, frequently with a membership drawn from two or three parishes, would provide a bier, a violet pall with a red cross worked on it, a white pall for the young, and would employ an undertaker or carpenter, who would work to the specifications of the guild. No black coverings were to be allowed on coffins, and mutes and feathers on horses were forbidden. The guiding principle was to deal with death in a devout and real manner, and avoid "all idle, vain displays of worldly pomp" and "all trifling and sentimentality".

Not all nineteenth-century burial guilds had the religious basis of Brett's. The majority were merely benefit clubs, intended to

help the poor meet the cost of funerals. The services provided by
such clubs were at times liable to abuse in a horrifying way as a
result of the exigencies of poverty. The *Catholic Weekly Instructor*
for 1845 records how in some places there was a positive premium
on the death of children:

> Soon after a child is born it is entered on the books of as many bury-
> ing clubs as the parents can command funds to pay for. The sum
> subscribed to each is but a few pence, or even halfpence weekly; so
> that parties being in full employment can sometimes afford to have
> the name on the register of ten or a dozen of these societies. And the
> investment may always be made a profitable one. The hapless child
> has to be killed by exposure, by neglect, and worse treatment, to give
> these unnatural parents a claim upon the several societies of which
> they have enrolled their infant a member, to the extent in all, perhaps,
> of 30, 40, or even 50.

Those who were concerned with the reform of funeral practice
were also concerned with the provision of suitable memorials.
Here again the attack was made against pagan emblems and unsuitable ostentation. At the beginning of the nineteenth century
the cross was rarely used on gravestones and memorial tablets, as
it was thought to be "popish". As a result most burial grounds
abounded in "Roman urns, funereal flames, Egyptian pyramids,
broken pillars, naked cupids with trumpets or inverted torches",
thus giving them, as the ecclesiologists recognized, a pagan
appearance. Some writers were so absolutely convinced that all
sepulchral monuments must have a symbolic meaning, that they
attempted to allegorize the classical monuments of earlier centuries. Thus William Sewell suggests that reclining figures on
sloping roofs and pyramids supported on four spheres were
intended to represent the instability of human affairs and the
proneness of human grandeur to fall. Theophilus Smith, who
produced a large number of suitable Gothick designs for
memorials, confessed to an inability to discover *any* symbolic
meaning in some of the classical designs—a failure which he
clearly regarded as worse than finding erroneous heathen symbolism in them. The ecclesiologists recommended "a Lom-
bardick Cross' as the most fitting memorial, with box trees
planted in the shape of a cross for those who could not afford a
stone memorial. Evangelicals also showed their concern for
appropriate memorials, though their attention was largely con-

centrated on the epitaphs. The *Christian Guardian* reveals the common belief of many Victorians that graveyards should be edifying places, by its castigation of the majority of epitaphs as ludicrous, unmeaning tributes, "indirectly pernicious in their moral tendency".

Epitaphs were, in fact, a favourite target for would-be reformers. The ecclesiologists urged avoidance of the word "died", because it expressed a non-Christian idea of finality, and hoped that the heresy of asserting the complete blessedness of the deceased would be avoided, humility shown, and a brief form adhered to. Various works were published containing selections of epitaphs adapted to different professions in society. Theophilus Smith included a section on them in his *Original Designs for Christian Memorials,* and E. Trollope's *Manual of sepulchral Monuments* lists suitable biblical quotations and fragments of poetry culled from Keble, Heber, and innumerable lesser-known sources. Despite the recommendation of brevity many of these are as long as some eighteenth-century epitaphs, though it is certainly true that nearly all are marked by a religious didacticism, a reference to death rather than to the achievements of the deceased, and the expression of hope in that favourite Victorian doctrine, the recognition and reunion of friends in heaven.

Besides the individual memorials attention was also given to their setting—the churchyard or cemetery. For the ecclesiologists vaults were a notorious evil, for they were reflections of the pew-rent system beyond death, whereby, not only the seats in church were apportioned amongst private individuals by rent, but the churchyard, the common resting-place of all men, was likewise alienated. Moreover, the erection of iron railings around the vault area made this class division obvious to all. The new cemeteries required cemetery chapels, and the ecclesiologists were not slow to put forward suggestions. The model which they considered the most appropriate was based on the church of the Holy Sepulchre at Jerusalem, having a circular nave, with a chancel and sanctuary a little longer than the diameter of the nave. The bier would then be placed in the centre of the nave, with the mourners ranged around it.

> The general character of the whole will be grave-sombre, for the portion of humanity is sorrow; but not dismal, for the sorrow of the Christian is full of hope. The windows save the one over the Altar,

will be small and few, and all will be filled with stained glass. The glare of day will be thus excluded, and a more fitting light will be created internally by the employment of solemn tapers. Round the walls will be hung pieces of dark-coloured tapestry, worked in suitable patterns, and frescoes will be painted above these. The subject for the stained glass in the east window may be the Resurrection, or the Final Doom. Memorials to the departed may occupy the side-lights. These and brasses will be the only monuments allowed in the public parts of the chapel.

Pugin, who shared the ecclesiologists' abhorrence of the pagan symbolism employed in memorials, designed a series of brasses depicting crinolined ladies in the most approved attitudes of medieval piety.

Others besides the ecclesiologists were concerned with the new cemeteries. The Unitarian minister of Lewin's Mead Chapel in Bristol urged that places of interment should be made places of attraction to mourners, secluded from the public thoroughfare, but still enough within the general view "to be a lesson of mortality to the living and unheeding crowd". J. C. Loudon, in a work of 1843 entitled *On the Laying-out, Planting and Managing of Cemeteries*, held that a burial ground had two functions:

> The main object . . . is the disposal of the remains of the dead in such a manner as that their decomposition and return to the earth from which they sprung shall not prove injurious to the living. . . . A secondary object is, or ought to be, the improvement of the moral sentiments and general taste of all classes and more especially of the great masses of society.

The aim of moral improvement had its roots in the long-standing *memento mori* tradition, but it soon assumed more secular forms, for many of the new cemeteries were planted out with rare trees, and some at least held that the encouragement of botanizing should be one of the functions of the new cemeteries. Loudon proposed that disused churchyards should be converted into cemetery gardens, and produced elaborate plans of leafy walks, and even of churchyards converted into neat rows of allotments in an agricultural parish. Inspiration was sometimes drawn from abroad and frequent mention is made of the solemn atmosphere produced by the innumerable cypresses of the great Muslim cemetery of Eyup, which lies at the head of the Golden Horn in Constantinople. The planners of the new cemeteries had some success in their endeavours to persuade the public to resort to them as parks. W. Leask noted in his memoirs that they were becoming favourite places of promenade because of their atmosphere of peaceful repose and urged that more thought should be given to ways of stressing the solemnity of death, so that the living might benefit.

Later in the century the garden-cemetery idea found advocates who favoured classical memorials once more. A notable exponent of this was W. Robinson, who in 1880 produced a short book, *God's Acre Beautiful, or the Cemeteries of the Future,* in which he depicted classical temple columbaria and statues of maidens weeping over urns, set amidst poplars and weeping willows and spacious lakes.

The 1870s saw a new factor emerging—the public discussion of cremation. The *Dublin Review* noted in 1876 that two years previously "all the talk of clubs and drawing rooms was tinged with funeral pyres and noxious exhalations", and that only now was it possible "to dine out without hearing any explicit reference to what the French call the *cinders* of one's forefathers". Investigations into the possibility of cremation had been proceeding on the Continent for some time before, but in England the discussion only became serious with the publication of an article by Sir Henry Thompson in the *Contemporary Review* advocating cremation. This led to the formation of a society known as "Urne" in 1874 to promote cremation and, in the following year, to the formation of the Cremation Society. Other suggestions for the disposal of the dead were made at the same time, including a scheme put forward by F. S. Hayden (in a tract entitled *Earth to Earth*) urging the burial of the dead in wicker coffins, with the corpse laid amidst evergreens, by which means, he suggested, the lowlands of Essex and Kent might be reclaimed if a sufficiently large number of burials took place there over the course of time. Sir Henry Thompson held that cremation could save the country £500,000 a year on imported bone meal, by the judicious use of the remains left over after cremation.

The legal doubts concerning cremation were finally dispelled by a judgement of Sir James Stephen in 1884, but it only very slowly won acceptance. For Christians the idea was tinged with pagan associations, and, considering how vehement had been the protests against the pagan symbolism of funerals earlier in the century, it is not surprising that there was strong opposition to cremation. Other arguments were adduced from the doctrine of the resurrection of the body—frequently understood in a very literal way—which some, such as Bishop Christopher Wordsworth, thought would be weakened in the public mind. Thus the development of cremation was left entirely in secular hands.

As far as churchyards and cemeteries are concerned, the nineteenth century, with its concern for edification of the living by the memorials of the dead, with its belief in "Christian architecture" and Gothick symbolism, and with its at best deeply serious, and at worst morbid, concern with death, has left its undoubted mark. Today its large, and frequently ugly, monuments, giving decaying testimony to numbers of uneminent Victorians, may serve as better reminders of the transitoriness of human life in their neglect than the elaborate inscriptions on them originally intended to convey just that message.

5

Towards a
Liturgy of Committal

W. Jardine Grisbrooke

In his editorial introduction to a recent number of the review
Concilium devoted to the theme "Death and Burial: Theology and
Liturgy", Heinrich Rennings points out that before a new burial
liturgy can be satisfactorily composed, or an old one satisfactorily
revised, it is necessary to consider

> . . . the theological content of what the Christian message has to say
> about dying, death, and "the last things" in general. For instance, is
> the description of death as a "separation of body and soul" satis-
> factory or misleading? Should this manner of speaking still occur in
> the liturgy's prayers? How should the liturgical texts express such
> realities of the faith as purgatory, heaven, hell, last judgment,
> resurrection, beatific vision, new heaven, new earth and others? Not
> merely in a way which is intelligible to people today and takes their
> prejudices into account, but so as to ensure that these realities appear
> to them for what they are: the unexpected fulfilment of their secret
> longings and a God-given certainty beyond all their guessing. One
> cannot expect prayers of the early Middle Ages to appeal to the
> modern Christian's understanding of creation and the world. That is
> why texts taken from ancient sources cannot by themselves provide
> a new liturgy. The fact that there are truths about dying, death, and
> resurrection which mean little or nothing to many people, forces us at
> least not to make the Christian message still more unintelligible by
> the use of unrealistic words and phrases. . . .[1]

A similar series of questions has been asked by Gilbert Cope in the
Introduction:

[1] *Concilium*, vol. 2, no. 4, February 1968, pp. 3-4.

... the narratives of the resurrection of Jesus and the various testimonies to experiences of the presence of the Risen Lord constitute
an irreplaceable heart in the Christian religion. How are they to be
understood today? Is there a modern theologically acceptable
alternative to the traditional view? Is there a corpus of belief called
"Christianity" which can survive such radical restatement and yet
remain recognizably the same in essence? ... Is it possible to devise
a rite which is theologically honest and yet does not give offence to
conventional Christians in their grief? Is the language of poetry and
the imagery of myth justifiable when reason and hope falter? What
are we to think about prayers for the dead and the meaning of heaven
and hell—not to mention purgatory and limbo?[1]

The first task of the liturgist who sets out to compile a liturgy
of committal is to establish the theology of death which his work
is to embody and express. The theology of death which is pre-
supposed in the rest of this essay is that expounded above by
Professor Hick[2] with only one important difference: in the light
of the exceedingly unpleasant forms which death so often takes,
and the distress which it causes whether its manner is unpleasant
or not, I am unable to reject the concept of a penal element in
death to the extent to which he rejects it; nor do I find any
difficulty in accommodating this neo-Augustinian element within
a generally neo-Irenean theology. In this matter I would dis-
tinguish between death as a universal natural phenomenon—
which I regard from a neo-Irenean standpoint—and death as it is
empirically known, which I can account for only as a consequence
of, and penalty for, sin.[3]

A Christian liturgy of committal, however, must embody and
express not only a Christian theology of death, but also a Christian
theology of *Christian* death. The principal characteristic of the
death of the Christian is that it is a participation in the death of
Christ. And because the *pasch* of Christ is one and indivisible, because his death cannot be separated from his resurrection, so also
the death of the Christian cannot be separated from *his* resurrection to come.

[1] Introduction, p. 2 and p. 5.
[2] "Towards a Christian Theology of Death", pp. 8–25, above.
[3] Compare Karl Rahner, *On the Theology of Death,* Section II. It might well
be asked, indeed, whether Irenaeus himself does not teach this also, and
whether, therefore, my use of "neo-Irenean", as well as Professor Hick's
omission of this element in his synthesis, is not begging the question.

Of vital importance to the liturgist is Professor Hick's insistence that any restatement of the fundamental Christian doctrines about the death and resurrection both of Christ and of the Christian, however radical, must be a restatement, and not an abandonment. Dr Cope asks whether it is "possible to devise a rite which is theologically honest and yet does not give offence to conventional Christians in their grief". I am sure that it is, and also that the first prerequisite of a theologically honest rite is that it should mean what it says. Nothing could be more dishonest, nor more likely to offend not only Christian mourners but anyone of intellectual integrity, than a funeral rite which made use of "the language of poetry and the imagery of myth" while evacuating that language and imagery of all real, objective meaning.

I do not deny the need for radical restatements. But I do deny the legitimacy of continuing to use the language of Christian conviction while asserting that that language does not represent objective fact, and of interpreting it in a way that deprives words of anything resembling their normal meaning. In the face of death and bereavement this kind of thing is as shabby morally as it is shoddy intellectually. Are the traditional Christian doctrines concerning the death and resurrection of Christ, the death and resurrection of the Christian, true—however much they may be in need of reformulation—or not? If not, no amount of poetry and imagery is of any use: there is no comfort, no hope, and we had better face the fact, and not attempt to evade its impact by playing games with words.

So there can be no soothing liturgy of committal which could be used by those who would evacuate Christian doctrine of all objective meaning. The only rite appropriate in such circumstances would be a utilitarian act of disposal of the corpse, accompanied by, at the most, a single word—"Amen".[1] Anything more would be meaningless. If I believe that it *is* possible to produce a liturgy of committal which is theologically honest today, and to produce one which will not give offence to Christian mourners, conventional or not, in their grief, it is because, thank God, I still believe —however falteringly at times—that the Christian hope *is* true.

[1] It is interesting to note that it would be possible to produce a much richer rite of committal on agnostic or even atheistic humanist principles: it is the curious attempt to hang on to belief in God without believing anything about him which leads one to the position of having nothing to say.

What are the truths about death in general, and about Christian death in particular, which should be embodied and expressed in a Christian liturgy of committal? First, that death is not something which happens to the body but does not affect the soul, even less a "deliverance" of an immortal soul from a mortal body, but something which involves the whole man, something which cannot be put right by anything short of what traditional theology calls "the resurrection of the body". Second, that except in the context of the death and resurrection of Christ death is indeed what it appears to be—the end. Third, that the death of the Christian is, like that of Christ, and because it is a participation in that of Christ, the preliminary to his glorification, a corporeal as well as a spiritual glorification. Fourth, that the Christian is a partaker in the death of Christ in his own dying because he has been a partaker in it in his own living, in baptism and the euchar- ist. All this is implicit in the paschal concept of Christian death, and so far as possible all this should be expressed in the liturgy of committal. Most of the liturgies of committal in current use fall very far short of giving it adequate expression, and the ways in which they are usually performed fall even shorter, especially in the almost complete absence of the note of paschal *triumph*. The restoration of this element in the Christian concept of death to its due place in the funeral liturgy is most important.

There is, however, another side to the death of the Christian, one which in certain periods of Christian history has been over- emphasized, but which should not for that reason now be under- emphasized. Just as the Christian's participation in the paschal mystery of Christ during his life is imperfect, so is his participation in it in death. He is not yet capable of receiving his final glorifica- tion. And the farther he travels on the road to glory, the farther also he travels on the road to judgement, for judgement is precisely self-revelation in the blazing light of glory. Ladislas Boros[1] has suggested that we think of the stage in the Christian journey which traditional western theology calls "purgatory" in terms of a "breaking through to clarity", and the concept seems to me to be a valuable one, capable of preserving the valid and necessary elements of a "purgatorial" doctrine of the Christian's progress between death and resurrection—and surely none can

[1] "Some Thoughts on the Four Last Things", in *Concilium,* loc. cit., pp. 38–42.

doubt the necessity of some such perfecting—while guarding against the possibility of interpreting it in a penal manner.

In order, then, to reflect adequately the paschal character of Christian death, *the liturgy of committal must be at once triumphant and penitential, confident and suppliant, exultant and restrained.* And this is not only theologically necessary: it accords also with both the spiritual and the psychological needs of the bereaved. For if an exaggeratedly sorrowful liturgy of committal—and such all too many existing ones are—is neither fitting theologically nor helpful psychologically, an exaggeratedly joyful one—such as some now seem inclined to produce by reaction[1]—is no better. What is needed is a liturgy in which the delicate balance between these two emphases is achieved and maintained.

We must now ask ourselves exactly what we mean when we speak of a liturgy of *committal*: who or what is committed, to whom or what, and by whom? The conventional answer to these questions would be that the soul of the deceased is committed to the hands of God, and his body to the earth, by the minister and mourners. Greater theological precision is called for than this statement of the matter implies, however, for it takes for granted that definition of death as the separation of the soul from the body with which many theologians are increasingly dissatisfied. For on the one hand it is intolerable to tell those who have known and loved a man that it is only "his body" that is dead, and that "he" is still alive elsewhere, as if he himself were something other than the man they have seen and touched, listened and spoken to, and theologically misleading as well, implying as it does a non-Christian idea of the relation of the soul to the body: and, on the other hand, it would seem equally inexact to regard the particular collection of chemical particles which happen to constitute his body at the time of his death as *being*, without further qualification, that body. There is a sense in which the whole man has died and is dead; and there is a sense in which the whole man has passed through and beyond death.

[1] Some—by no means all—features of the experimental funeral liturgy now in use in the Roman Catholic archdiocese of Chicago seem to fall into this category. For an account of this rite see Theodore Stone and Anselm Cunningham, "The Chicago Experimental Funeral Rite", in *Concilium,* loc. cit., pp. 49–52.

Either way, it is the whole man, the whole person, who is committed to the care of God in this rite: and this must be made clear. And he is committed by the minister and the mourners not merely in their capacity as individuals who have known and loved him, but as members of the Church of which he also was and is a member, as members one of another in the Body of Christ. It is a profound theological realization of the indissoluble unity in Christ of the living and the departed that underlies the provision in all the historic Christian rites, but above all in the ancient Spanish and the Byzantine, of funeral psalms and anthems which only make sense when it is understood that it is the deceased who is uttering them. In other texts the community addresses its departed member: and this too is an expression of a real personal relationship, which death cannot destroy. Here, surely, is a liturgical emphasis which, carefully adapted and expressed, could be very meaningful indeed to us today, with our great concern for personal and relational values.

It is, of course, the same profound conviction which underlies the practice of praying for the departed, the inclusion of which in any liturgy of committal, as the expression of that trust and hope in God which *is* committal, is equally necessary theologically and psychologically. Theologically, if we are to think of death, as Professor Hick has suggested, as a halting-place on a man's journey to God, and if we are to think of him progressing farther on that journey beyond death, it is a demand of Christian love to pray for him after death just as much as it is to pray for him before it. Psychologically, nothing is more effective nor more valuable a part of ministry to the bereaved than this, as is evident from the all but universal practice of it throughout human history.

There are, of course, those who object to prayer for the dead. To those who object because, as adherents of the New Reformation, they doubt or deny the value of *any* intercessory prayer, whether for the living or for the departed, I can only repeat what I have already said in another context—that, however much some of the fundamental doctrines and practices of Christianity are in need of radical reformulation, reformulation is one thing and abandonment is another. With those who object on the familiar grounds of the Old Reformation I am unable to debate the subject, because I have never been able to make sense of their arguments: I can only regard them as a psychologically understandable, but completely illogical, reaction against the distortions of the late medieval church in the other direction—a reaction which not only leaves intact but actually magnifies the error upon which those distortions were founded, the application of the conditions of time and space outside time and space. But I must add that if, as a theologian, I find this refusal to pray for the departed so illogical as to be incomprehensible, as an ordinary Christian I find the refusal to let others pray for them, which it nearly always seems to involve, so uncharitable as to be immoral. The comment of a distinguished Methodist minister on this unchristian aberration is very much to the point:

> . . . Protestant Christianity has not very much to say to any Christian who has been through the crucial experience of seeing the face he loves most in the world recede into the inaccessible mystery of death. The embarrassed silence we offer the bereaved (who usually and naturally want very much to talk about their beloved dead) is outrageous—the stone with which our scepticism and inadequate sympathy respond to their request for bread.[1]

If a liturgy of committal which does not adequately express the paschal character of Christian death is no more than half Christian, one which deprives the bereaved even of the consolation of praying with and for those from whom death has separated them is not Christian at all.

What should be the content of prayers for the dead? The principal emphasis throughout should be upon the ultimate resurrection and glorification. But there is no reason to abandon the traditional petitions for light, peace, rest, refreshment, and so forth: and if we conceive of the time between death and resurrection primarily as a time for further journeying, we may see in them a richness of meaning which has largely been lost in their conventional use.[2]

The other aspect of committal is the reverent disposal of the body. But if we interpret the doctrine of the resurrection of the body in a way compatible with science—and it should, perhaps, be pointed out that this is not a "new" issue: our ancestors knew

---

[1] J. Neville Ward, *The Use of Praying* (1967), p. 96.

[2] The description of the present state of the faithful departed as a 'sleep in Christ' which is found in ancient liturgical documents does not appear to imply a state of unconsciousness, for it is often found in conjunction with these and similar petitions.

just as well as we do what happens to dead bodies, even if they did not explain the chemical processes in the same language—is this anything more than a mere disposal of waste matter, however reverently it must be done for the sake of the bereaved? Is it in any real sense a "committal"? Yes, it is, for two reasons.

First, it is an acknowledgement of God's dominion, the formal return to him of that which he gave—"The Lord gave, and the Lord has taken away: blessed be the name of the Lord." The formal surrender of the body is the final sign of the self-surrender of the whole man to God, that self-surrender in trust and hope and love which is the essence both of "commitment" and of "committal". Second, this acknowledgement takes the form of a committal of created matter to created matter. In one way or another the body is returned whence it came. It is a truism to say that in nature death in some form is a necessary precondition of life, but it is one that is worth remembering in this context, and in the light of it the committal of the body to the natural element of earth or water or fire may be seen to be closely related to the expectation of further life.

In both ways, then, the physical committal of the body is the sign and symbol of the committal of the whole man to God, his Creator, and as such it is not merely a necessary but theologically a significant part of the liturgy of committal, in which this significance must be made clear.

Many funeral services, and related rites, are in use in the Christian Church today, and there are others which are no longer in use, and they cannot be ignored by the liturgical reviser attempting to construct a liturgy of committal which may be more appropriate to present needs. Indeed, one approach to the task would be to examine the rites in contemporary use, assessing their merits and demerits, and then suggest ways in which they might be revised in accordance with the current renewal of a more profound theology of death and with contemporary needs. Alternatively, it would be possible to approach the problem from the historical angle, tracing the development of Christian funeral rites, noting where and when and why important changes have occurred, assessing the significance of these changes, and then attempting to construct a liturgy of committal in the light of what had been learned in this way.

I have in fact worked through the problem in both these ways, but I do not intend to describe the process now. I propose instead to consider, first, the general principles upon which a liturgy of committal should be based; second, in very general terms, the pattern and content of the kind of liturgy which would arise from applying these principles, and the manner of its performance; and third, two closely related issues—the manner and the place of committal and disposal.

The first general principle which should be borne in mind throughout is *flexibility*. The variety of circumstances and consequently of needs which must be provided for in a liturgy of committal today is greater than ever before. In the Middle Ages, for example, there was to all intents and purposes a single pattern of burial rite. The body was taken to the parish church, where the various offices which composed the funeral liturgy were celebrated, and from there it was borne into the churchyard for burial. Today we have to provide for a service in the village church followed by burial in the village churchyard, as of old; for a service in an urban or suburban church, followed by burial in a distant cemetery; for a service in a church, followed by cremation at a distant crematorium; for a service as well as the cremation at the crematorium; and for several other combinations of this kind. Before the service, the body may be in the house, or in a hospital, or in a church, or in a funeral director's chapel. And all this is complicated—especially in the great conurbations—by problems of transport. All this must be taken into account: the liturgy must be flexible enough to fit any of these circumstances.

Moreover, it must be flexible enough to fit them in an orderly and satisfying way. So our second principle is what may be called *adequacy*. Within this flexibility every contingency, every need, spiritual and psychological as well as practical, must be provided for, and provided for adequately. This is a vital part of the Church's ministry to the bereaved, and also of the Church's witness. The inadequacy of our present funeral services cannot but confirm the "four-wheel Christian", who only comes to church for christenings, weddings, and funerals, in his belief that he is not missing anything by not coming at any other time, while to the practising Christian it can be a cause of considerable emotional and spiritual distress. Any liturgy of committal, then, must be so constructed that it will provide as strong a safeguard as possible against this kind of inadequacy. It must be *humanly* adequate, responding to the needs of the bereaved, and it must be *Christianly* adequate as well, conveying the Christian message about death as clearly and fully as possible, whatever the circumstances in which it is performed.

This it can only do if its theological content is as full as possible, and if the liturgical embodiment of that content is as rich as possible. And this means that we must follow the pattern of the great historic liturgies, which provide a number of funeral offices, rather than that of the liturgies stemming from the Reformation, which commonly provide only a single funeral service of a very jejune kind. A single office cannot possibly provide either the flexibility which is practically necessary or the theological fullness and liturgical richness which are humanly and Christianly necessary.

The funeral services of the great historic rites themselves, however, do not answer our present needs as they stand. Their theological emphases, as distinct from their theological foundations, are those of another age, and so, of course, is the imagery of their language; and therefore they fail to speak to us in the way in which they spoke to those who compiled and used them long ago. They have come to lose, in modern use, the three notes which together constitute the third general principle upon which a liturgy of committal for today must be constructed: *simplicity*, *clarity*, and *intelligibility*.

Simplicity is *not* the same thing as starkness, bareness, or meanness—although these are often dignified with the name, to which they have no right at all. Simplicity, in a liturgical context, means directness unobscured by fuss, the exclusion of all meaningless minor elaboration—for just as bareness is not the same thing as simplicity, so elaboration is not the same thing as richness. Simplicity and richness are by no means incompatible, and both are vital to the quality which is necessary if the theological message and the spiritual impact of the liturgy are to be conveyed effectively—clarity.

But clarity demands also logical order, and this is something which has been too often absent from funeral services in the last few centuries.[1] Logical order is well exemplified in the aims of

---

[1] The medievals, whom it is now so fashionable to despise, handled the matter far better, see pp. 77–8, below.

those who compiled the liturgy of committal now authorized for experimental use in the Roman Catholic archdiocese of Chicago.

A vigilant attempt has been made to so structure the rite that it moves towards a climax, from the vigil beginning with recognition of sorrow and loss, then to the meeting of the body at the door of the church reminiscent of the day of baptism, then to the eucharistic liturgy to relate the Eucharist to the death and life of the Christian, then to the final commendation as a fitting prelude to the procession from the church marking the triumph over death, and finally to the ceremony at the cemetery at which the mourners look forward to final resurrection and parousia.[1]

This is a very well thought-out expression of the significance of death in the Christian life, and one which corresponds very closely to the liturgical implications of Professor Hick's concept of death as a staging-point on a journey. The theological content of our liturgy of committal will be marked by a progression of thought of this kind.

The importance of intelligibility has been clearly and succinctly expressed in the Constitution on the Sacred Liturgy of the Second Vatican Council:

The purpose of the sacraments is to sanctify men, to build up the body of Christ and finally to give worship to God; because they are signs they also instruct. They not only presuppose faith, but by words and objects they also nourish, strengthen and express it; that is why they are called "sacraments of faith". They have indeed the power to impart grace, but, in addition, the very act of celebrating them effectively disposes the faithful to receive this grace fruitfully, to worship God duly and to love each other mutually. It is therefore of the highest importance that the faithful should easily understand the sacramental signs. . . .[2]

And this, of course, applies to all the services of the Church, not only to sacraments and sacramentals.

Intelligibility involves three things. First, simplicity, accuracy, and reasonable modernity of language. Second, care in the use of imagery and mythology: it is pointless to indulge in a wealth of linguistic imagery which, however traditional it may be, is not likely to mean much to the great majority of the worshippers to whom it is offered. Third, however, to attain intelligibility it is

---

[1] The article cited in p. 61, footnote (p. 51).   [2] loc. cit., art. 59.

essential to resist what the late Bishop Hensley Henson once called "the lust for intelligibility". It is possible to modernize the language of the liturgy so injudiciously, or so to mistake colloquialism for modernity, that the result not only lacks that dignity which is as vital to intelligibility as are simplicity and accuracy, but will also be intolerably dated, and require further revising, within ten or twenty years. Again, while it is important that the liturgy should not be overloaded with imagery which cannot be understood, it is equally important that it should not be so emptied of content under the pretext of "demythologizing" that there is nothing left in it to understand. It must also be borne in mind that the intelligibility essential to the liturgy is not of a merely intellectual kind, and that it will not be achieved if what may be called the element of poetry is excluded, either from the substance of what is said, or from the way in which it is said; nor is it an intelligibility which can be at once manifest to everyone who may happen to be present.

These last two points deserve further consideration. In his contribution above, Dr Mathers has pointed out that, from a psychologist's angle, one of the gravest problems connected with death in contemporary society is our lack of community sense, and consequently of true community behaviour. As a liturgist, I can only agree with him, and I must add that in this context Christians must face the facts: Our society is no longer Christian, and the rites of the Christian community, therefore, cannot be, and cannot be made, directly intelligible to the majority of our contemporaries. Some of the problems of liturgical renewal would be greatly simplified if this were recognized. It is the task of the liturgical reviser to produce services which are intelligible to the worshiping community, and which, *so far as is possible,* will manifest the nature of the worship and of the community to those on the fringes of it, or entirely outside it: but it is not his task to attempt the impossible, and to try to produce Christian services which will be directly intelligible to non-Christians. If he does try to do this, he will only succeed in making them less intelligible than ever, as well as totally inadequate. It is possible to explain the meaning of liturgical services constructed upon clear and rational principles; it is not possible to explain the meaning of anything from which all meaning has been removed, for whatever reason. It is no task of the liturgist to attempt in this futile way to make up for the failure of the clergy to preach the gospel which they are commissioned to preach. The Christian liturgy is the worship of the Christian community, and a community which exists for specific purposes inevitably has to *explain* the ways in which it fulfils those purposes to those who are not members of it.[1]

This was the situation of the early Christians, and to cope with it they provided thorough courses of instruction. This is the position of Christians today; and to suppose that it can be short-circuited is to manifest an unhealthy nostalgia for a period in Christian history which has passed. I must make it clear, then, that when I consider the problem of compiling a Christian liturgy of committal for today I am not concerned to produce some vague half-Christian rite which can be used over the bodies of vague half-Christians. A Christian liturgy of committal must, by definition, be a liturgy to be used by Christians for committing the souls and bodies of departed Christians—and in both cases this means *practising, worshipping* Christians: it is only when all that this involves has been thoroughly considered, and the results embodied in liturgical rites, that it *may* be possible to produce rites to be used by Christians for committing the souls and bodies of the half-Christians of whom our society is at present largely composed.

And just as it is wrong, and indeed absurd, to envisage producing a liturgy of committal in which the Christian mourner would be deprived of consolation, and the Christian Church of witness, in order to make it usable by and for half-Christians or even non-Christians, so it is equally wrong, and equally absurd, to deprive the man who needs beauty, drama, poetry, in his worship—and above all at a time of bereavement—of the great consolation which these gifts of God afford, in order to make the

[1] I cannot enter here into the current theological controversy about the relationship of the Church to the world, but can only record my own adherence to the traditional concept of the Church as a particular society which exists in and for, but is not identical with, society as a whole. There are those today who manifest something very like panic in their concern that the Church shall not appear to be an "in-group": but any community which has conditions of membership is by definition an "in-group"! It is time, indeed, that this phrase were dropped, for it is not at all clear that those who use it know what they mean by it, apart from treating it as a pejorative equivalent of "community"—if you like a group of people you describe them as a community, and if you don't you describe them as an in-group.

liturgy of committal more immediately and more superficially comfortable for the man who, consciously and apparently (for in this context the needs of the unconscious and subconscious man must be remembered), has no need of these things. To produce a kind of liturgical highest common factor is to injure and insult both the man who is a committed practising Christian and the man who is not, the man of sensibility as well as the man who appears to lack it. There is no place whatever in liturgical renewal for what may be called liturgical iconoclasm, and this is true above all when we are dealing with the liturgy of committal.

The first rite which ought to be provided is one which might be used, should it be desired, to accompany those things which, for decency and reverence, must be done to the body after death. Anciently, three acts in this preparation of the body for burial were regarded as having theological significance and were given liturgical form: washing, anointing or embalming, and clothing. These actions are now normally performed in a purely practical manner by nurses or undertakers, but this ritual provision should be restored, for it could have a threefold value today. First, in certain circumstances, it could be a very effective part of the ministry to the bereaved. Second, it could express in a direct and telling way certain important truths about the nature of the Christian community and the coinherence of individual Christians in that community: for such a rite, properly constructed and performed, would be a most moving symbol of the Christian commitment to mutual love and service. Third it could also serve to proclaim, at the very beginning of the funeral rites, the paschal character of Christian death. In the historic liturgies, as they were originally performed, and as they still could and should be performed, washing, anointing, and clothing are intimately connected in the rites of Christian initiation. The paschal character of Christian death, as we have already seen, derives precisely from the paschal character of Christian initiation. So, when a man's earthly life is ended, the washing, anointing, and clothing of his body, by or in the presence of his relatives and friends, might remind them forcibly of the foundation of the Christian hope, of the incorporation into Christ, the risen and glorified Saviour, which is the gate by which the Christian has already entered into life eternal. Of course, a rite such as this

would not have the same impact if the rites of initiation themselves are celebrated, as at present is all but universal, in a liturgically impoverished and psychologically unsatisfactory manner.
But the answer to this difficulty is obvious.[1]

The theological symbolism of a rite of this kind is of a secondary
nature, but this does not invalidate it, nor does it render it less
effective and edifying. It is necessary to prepare the body for
committal; and it is surely right and proper that this should be
done in a way calculated to console and edify the bereaved. It may
be objected, however, that a large number of people today would
not find such a rite consoling or edifying, but might rather be
distressed by it. The answer to this is threefold. First, no one
would be forced to use it: as I have already made clear, a liturgy
of committal should provide for every likely need in every likely
set of circumstances, and in such a way that those parts of it which
are not needed in a particular instance may be omitted without
thereby diminishing the value of the other parts. This particular
rite, unless and until the idea of it were generally accepted, would
normally be omitted, but it should be available for those who
desire it. Second, the very existence of such a rite might well be a
valuable instrument in re-educating people towards a psychologically and theologically sounder attitude to death. Third, what
people think they want, and what they actually need, are often
very different things. There is no aspect of our present funeral
customs which is more unsatisfactory than the way in which, by
one means or another, we increasingly seek to help people to
evade the awful impact of the reality of death, instead of helping
them to do what in the end they *have* to do, which is to face it and
to cope with it. When I find that a rite of this kind, in one form or
another, has been a part of funeral customs almost universally
throughout human history, I cannot but conclude that it corresponds to a fundamental human need, and that the absence of it
may be psychologically dangerous. And I think we might well be
surprised, were we to provide it, and gently to teach people about
it and encourage them to use it, to find how soon and how widely
it would come to be accepted and valued.

The body having thus been prepared for committal, and the
bereaved having been prepared for it in this gentle, quiet, and

[1] We are here confronted with an instance of the impossibility of piecemeal
liturgical reform.

intimate manner, we have next to ask whether we should provide any further offices before the funeral services themselves. I think we should. Once more, we must recognize and provide an outlet for an all but universal natural instinct, the desire to pray by the body of a departed loved one—a desire which is often manifested far beyond the limited circles of those who regularly go to church, or who habitually pray at any other time. It might be manifested much more widely still were we to provide people with some help to do it. It may be asked why this provision should take a liturgical form: cannot those who wish to pray at this time do so less formally in an extempore way? There is nothing to stop those who are able and wish to do this from doing so; but experience suggests that, especially at a time of bereavement, people are very thankful for the help and guidance of clear and simple liturgical forms. And this is particularly true of those who are not used to praying at other times.

What form should this assistance take? I would suggest that we provide short offices, of the type which is provided for this and many other purposes in the historic rites, composed basically of a relevant psalm, and a *short* relevant reading from the scriptures, with the Lord's Prayer, and one or two other prayers, realistic, simple and direct. The tone of these offices should be one of quiet Christian confidence—that confidence which is an amalgam of penitence, hope, and trust. And the psalms, readings, and prayers should be selected and integrated with the greatest care, with respect for that logical progression of thought of which I have already written, and with an imaginative appreciation of the needs of mourners today.

These short offices could, of course, be used anywhere, according to circumstances—in the home, in church, in a hospital chapel, in a funeral director's chapel. But before we can consider the pattern of the actual funeral services themselves, we must consider the place of repose of the body between death and the funeral, and the place of committal. The relevance of these to the arrangements of the funeral liturgy may be apparent if I list at this stage what I believe should be the component parts of the latter:

1. An office of reception at the church door or church gate.
2. A vigil office, or "wake".
3. The eucharist.

4. A ceremony of "farewell".
5. The committal procession.
6. The committal itself.

A very little reflection will suffice to show that this arrangement, which is both the most traditional and the most logical, can
only be followed without adaptation if the body is brought to the
church at the very latest during the evening preceding the day of
the funeral, and if the committal takes the form of burial in a
churchyard or cemetery close at hand. This, which was once the
norm, is now the exception.

The present almost universal custom of taking the body from
the place of death, wherever that may be, to a funeral director's
chapel, and leaving it there until the actual funeral, creates a
considerable difficulty. For not only is it impossible, in these
circumstances, to celebrate the vigil or wake at the proper time
and in the proper place; it is practically impossible to celebrate it at
all, for it is inconvenient, for a number of reasons, to celebrate it
in the funeral director's chapel, however dignified a place of
repose that may be. Two other considerations reinforce my
conviction that this practice is one that should be discouraged,
and the necessary facilities provided in the church building. First,
it deprives those members of the Christian community who wish
to pray by the body before the funeral of the opportunity of doing
so. Second, it is intimately connected with what I have already
described as "the way in which, by one means or another, we
increasingly seek to help people to evade the awful impact of the
reality of death, instead of helping them to do what in the end
they *have* to do, which is to face it and to cope with it". The vast
majority of funeral directors treat the bodies placed in their
keeping with the greatest reverence; but most of them would
probably agree that one of the strongest motives which leads
people to accept this arrangement is the superficial desire to have
as little to do with the dead body as possible. In the home or in the
church its presence is evident and powerful; in the funeral
director's chapel it is shut away where it cannot disturb anyone.
Every church, then, should be provided with a chapel of rest,
conveniently arranged and appropriately adorned for this purpose, and the body should be taken there at the very latest on the
evening preceding the funeral.

In enumerating the parts of the funeral liturgy I did not include the procession or journey *to* the church, as distinct from that from the church to the place of committal. Unlike the latter, the former appears never to have assumed a theological as distinct from a practical character in the funeral liturgy, and the reason for this is not far to seek; it has no symbolical function, for the last journey of the Christian is *from* the Church in this age to that in the next, and to invest the journey *to* the church building with any theological meaning would be to destroy any logical progression in the theological content of the funeral rites. In the historic rites, in which during the middle ages formularies were provided for every possible action, material is supplied for use on the journey to the church, and should it be required today could be used without much change: in the west it consists merely of appropriate psalms. But it is not likely to be required very often in modern conditions.

The vigil office, or "wake", appears to correspond to some deep-felt need: it is remarkable how frequently, when no liturgical provision is made for it, some social substitute for it has been found. It has nearly always taken the form of a series of scripture readings accompanied or interspersed with appropriate psalms or responsorial singing drawn from the psalms or other parts of scripture, together with a small number of prayers based upon the instructive and meditative matter. This still seems to be the most suitable material: its arrangement is a matter for experiment and there is no reason why uniformity should be either desired or expected. Those concerned to experiment in this way would need to familiarize themselves thoroughly with the forms the service has taken in the past, and with existing modern versions of it, such as that in use in the archdiocese of Chicago.

But *the* service by and in which the Christian community bids farewell and godspeed to its departed member, just as it is *the* service by and in which it expresses all it needs to say and do at any other important stage in the Christian life, communal or individual, is the eucharist. The eucharist is the central and principal part of the liturgy of committal in the scheme here envisaged, not an optional extra for the specially devout, and in so far as any one part of the scheme corresponds to the single "funeral service" of common current practice it is the eucharist.

Although the eucharist has been celebrated as part of the actual funeral liturgy during the greater part of Christian history in the

greater part of Christendom, there have been and still are many
exceptions to this practice even in the historic rites themselves.
Throughout Eastern Christendom today, for example, it is more
usual for the funeral eucharist to be celebrated independently of
the liturgy of committal, sometimes on the same day, sometimes
on another day.[1] And this appears to have been the custom at one
time in the ancient Roman rite.[2] But deliberately to follow this
usage, as one or two Roman Catholic theologians now advocate,[3]
rather than to follow that which has prevailed in the Roman rite
for many centuries of celebrating it as part of the liturgy of
committal itself, would be to indulge in theological and liturgical
archaeologizing at the expense of pastoral realism. For if the
eucharist is to be celebrated in this context at all, which the renewed emphasis on the paschal character of Christian death seems
to me to require as an absolute *sine qua non* of a Christian liturgy
of committal, then it should be the central and fundamental part
of that liturgy. In the first place, the eucharist by its very nature
must be the central and fundamental act of any Christian liturgical
complex which includes it: to retain a funeral eucharist but to
separate it from the rest of the liturgy of committal is to devalue
the latter. Second, the funeral eucharist is the final summary of
the eucharistic life of the departed Christian, the final paschal act
which sets a seal upon the paschal life which has gone before.
Third, it is the act by which the Church on earth both proclaims
and recreates its abiding communion in Christ with its departed
member. It is the earthly foretaste of that heavenly banquet to
which all Christians, whether at any one time they be living or
departed, are called. Fourth, it is the act, the only act, in which all
thanksgiving, all prayer, on this occasion, as on any other, can be
and is summed up utterly and completely. And because it is all
these things it is also, fifth, the supreme ministry of consolation
to the bereaved.

For these reasons the eucharist must be the central, the principal,
the fundamental, part of the liturgy of committal, to which all that

[1] Among the Greeks, and to a lesser extent among the Slavs, in modern
times it is often omitted altogether, its place being taken by short devotional
offices of intercession for the departed. But this is a corruption, with which I
am not concerned.

[2] See the article by Damien Sicard, "Should there be a Funeral Mass?" in
Concilium, loc. cit., pp. 22–5.

[3] E.g. by Damien Sicard, loc. cit.

precedes it leads, and from which all that follows it derives its meaning and value. All this wealth of meaning which is inherent in the funeral eucharist must be brought out as fully, clearly, and sensitively as possible in the choice of readings, anthems, prayers, psalms, hymns, and so on, and a considerable selection of these is required, that they may be appropriate in many varying circumstances.[1]

In discussions of funeral customs, reference is often made to the necessity for a "suitable ceremony of farewell", and it is asserted that the lack of such a ceremony in our current funeral rites in this country is one of the most frequent causes of distress to the bereaved: certainly, from my own experience of other funeral customs in which such a rite is a normal and integral part, I can bear witness to its value. What form might such a ceremony take? The one that comes at once to my mind, partly because of my own experience of it, partly because of its frequent recurrence in many different cultures and religions, which reflects, it seems to me, its ability to satisfy this particular need, is the "last kiss", which still survives as the most moving and best loved part of the funeral rites of Eastern Christendom. As the last act of the service in church —that is, in the scheme I am suggesting, after the eucharist—all those who wish to do so approach the coffin, which has been left open throughout the service, and kiss the hands or head of the departed.

The suggestion of so radical a change—even if it be only an optional one—from current English custom clearly needs justification. Of course, I am not under any illusion that there is anything edifying, even less consoling, about looking at a body gravely or grossly disfigured, whether by disease or by injury. But this situation apart, and given the right circumstances (and it is our business to *make* the circumstances of a funeral right), I am sure that the open coffin is both extremely edifying and supremely consoling. I have myself been present, on more than one occasion, at a funeral liturgy conducted over the open coffin, and including the last kiss, with a largely English congregation totally unused to it and mostly unprepared for it, and the result has been vastly different from what one might in theory expect. I have seen, and sometimes heard, the surprise, and momentary alarm, giving way to an unexpected relief, and the relief to something which I

[1] See, e.g., the provisions of the Chicago experimental rite, outlined in *Concilium*, loc. cit., pp. 51–2.

cannot describe except in terms of Christian paschal joy in the face of death and the midst of bereavement, in one person after another confronted for the first time with these customs. Of course there are exceptions: there are always exceptions. But in general my experience leads me to answer the doubts and fears which I am sure will be the general reaction to this suggestion in the only way in which I can answer them: try it, and see.[1]

If the service in the church is conducted over an open coffin, it is of course necessary to close it (except in one circumstance, which I will consider later)—and it is not difficult to do this simply, swiftly, and reverently—before the next part of the liturgy of committal, the procession or journey to the churchyard, cemetery, or crematorium. The committal procession after the service, as distinct from the journey to church before it, was anciently regarded as an integral and important part of the liturgy. It was almost always and everywhere a triumphal, not a mournful, procession: in the ancient Roman rite, for example, the bier, borne on the shoulders of the bearers, was preceded and followed by men carrying lighted torches, and escorted by others bearing branches of palm and olive as tokens of victory,while the paschal "Alleluia!" was repeated again and again in the accompanying chants. And we have similar evidence from Syria, North Africa, and other countries, as well. In our own land this note of triumph and confidence still marked the procession from the church to the grave in the churchyard, and the actual committal, right down to the Reformation, whatever secondary trappings of a more mournful nature popular usage may have added in the later middle ages: on the way to the grave the paschal Psalm 113 (114), *When Israel came out of Egypt*, was sung, followed at the ceremonial opening of the grave by Psalm 117 (118), *O give thanks unto the Lord for he is gracious: for his mercy endureth for ever*, at the actual committal by Psalm 41 (42), *Like as the hart desireth the waterbrooks*, with a particularly triumphant accompanying anthem, and after the committal by Psalm 131 (132), *Lord, remember David*—quieter, as befitted the moment, but no less confident.[2] A careful examination

---

[1] Of course, such an innovation should only be made with the greatest care and discretion, both liturgical and pastoral.

[2] In the earlier pre-Conquest funeral rites even more triumphant texts were used, based on Psalm 23 (24), vv. 7–10. It may be as well to note here that a great deal of what is often said about medieval religion in self-consciously

of these psalms, and of the ceremonies which they accompanied
reveals an outstanding sureness of touch in those responsible for
the arrangement. We might do worse than use this as our starting
point in attempting to work out our committal procession and act
of committal.

But, of course, considerable structural adaptation is necessary.
A rite of this kind, as it stands, presupposes a procession from the
church to a nearby grave in the churchyard. We have to provide
for a variety of circumstances. We do not, in most instances,
proceed straight from the church into the churchyard as the
medievals did; nor are we able to hold liturgical funeral processions through the streets of our cities as the ancient Roman
rite envisaged. Moreover, in an increasing number of cases we do
not bury at all, but cremate, and our existing crematoria are not
adapted to functions of this kind. Indeed, it does not seem possible
to consider the committal procession without at the same time
examining the modes of committal to which it must lead.

We have to provide for three methods of committal at present:
burial, which for a reason which will emerge in a moment may be
called "burial in the modern manner"; cremation followed by
interment or some other form of preservation of the ashes;
cremation followed by scattering or some other form of destruction or dispersal of the ashes. To these a fourth should be added
for consideration: burial in the medieval manner—it would have
to be adapted, of course, but this could be done—without all the
modern trappings, and notably without a coffin. Let us first consider cremation.

Until recently—very recently indeed in the Roman Catholic
Church, and still in the Eastern Orthodox Church—cremation
has been absolutely forbidden, or at least strongly discouraged, by
Christian authorities:

> Cremation has always been abhorrent to Christian feeling, and
> though it was contended that the fate of the immortal soul was not
> affected by the mode of disposal of the body, there can be little
> doubt that the real cause of the revolt against the funeral pyre is to
> be found in the doctrine of the resurrection of the flesh.[1]

"progressive" theological and liturgical circles today is not in accord with
the historical evidence, and is of value only as a testimony to the inadequate
acquaintance with facts of those who say it.

[1] E. O. James, *Christian Myth and Ritual* (1933), p. 190.

During the early years of the modern movement for cremation this objection to the practice was reinforced by the openly anti-Christian motives of some of its advocates. It is not possible to dismiss this long-standing Christian objection to cremation as unreasonable, although one may regard it as exaggerated. The ancients and the medievals, after all, as already remarked, knew just as well as we do what happens to dead bodies: they were as aware as we are that the doctrine of the resurrection of the flesh cannot imply the resuscitation of the particular organization of chemicals which constitutes the body at the time of death, although they would not have put it in those words. The fact is that cremation has, historically, commonly gone hand in hand with a denial of *any* survival or resurrection of the individual person as such at all, however illogical this connection may be. And only a very rash man would attempt to deny that the modern revival of cremation in our culture has gathered momentum in direct proportion with the growth of disbelief in any form of life after or beyond death. All this notwithstanding, Christian theologians, and the authorities of Christian Churches, are surely wise in their increasing recognition that there is no intrinsic connection between cremation and such a disbelief, and therefore no *essential* theological objection to cremation itself in a Christian context.

Nevertheless, cremation as at present practised in this country is hardly appropriate as a Christian form of disposal of the dead. No problem need arise over the service or services: there is nothing whatever to prevent this taking place in church if the crematorium Chapel is, as they nearly all are, liturgically unsuitable and inconvenient. Nor is there any serious difficulty about adapting the committal procession to the needs of this situation: the matter to be sung or said can perfectly well be arranged to fit the two ends of the journey from the church to the crematorium, and part sung as the body is taken out of the church, part as it is taken into the crematorium for the ceremony of committal. Nor is it impossible to provide a really suitable verbal form of committal, instead of merely adapting one from the entirely different circumstances of burial. But the committal itself presents a serious difficulty theologically and liturgically.

As in burial the consigning of the body to the earth is the committal, so in cremation the consigning of the body to fire is the committal. And there can only be *one* act of committal: the committal, it will be recalled, is the act in which the final surrender of the body to the created element of earth or water or fire symbolizes the final surrender of the whole man to God his Creator. But what happens in cremation today? The ceremonial committal in the crematorium chapel is in fact not a committal at all: it is nearly always a sham ceremony, even when it does not take the absurd form of an artificial imitation of burial. For the *words* of committal are spoken: and everyone knows that in fact the *act* of committal has not taken place. Cremation is not an appropriate form of Christian committal unless and until it can be contrived that the ritual act of committal is real—that is, unless and until crematoria are planned and constructed to allow direct and immediate committal to the furnace as part of the service.[1]

A second difficulty arises from the fact that the cremation is not total, that there is a residue which has to be disposed of after cremation. This creates what may be called the problem of the double committal: to cremate after the funeral liturgy; and then to have a later committal of the residual matter is again to deprive the ritual and ceremonial committal of reality, in a different way. For the committal must be the *final* act; and at present the committal before cremation is not the final act—something else has to be done afterwards, and that something else inevitably constitutes a second, and liturgically and psychologically indefensible, committal. A second improvement on existing practice, then, is required if cremation is to be appropriate in a Christian liturgy of committal: the actual process of cremation must be perfected so that the body is *completely* consumed by fire.[2]

If—and only if—these conditions could be fulfilled cremation would be an appropriate form of Christian committal. Even so, it

[1] The reader will notice that Mr Bond, in his paper on the architecture of crematoria, advocates precisely the same thing, and expounds the mechanics of its provision. Mr Bond and I had never met before this conference, and had no knowledge of the contents of one another's papers. The same conclusion appears to me to follow also from Dr Mathers' paper, the contents of which, again, were unknown either to Mr Bond or to myself. I suggest that the way in which the considerations adduced by a theologian, a psychologist, and an architect all tend, quite independently, to the same conclusion is a strong argument in favour of its validity.

[2] In the discussion following this paper it was stated, by an authority on the subject, that this was in fact likely to be achieved within the next fifteen years.

would not be the *most* appropriate form. Indeed, of the three possible elements which can be used as the vehicle of committal—earth, water, and fire—fire is the least appropriate, and both earth and water are to be preferred to it, for in committal to either there is an inherent natural symbolism of death and rebirth, of creation and re-creation, of dissolution and resurrection, which is not only theologically fitting but also scientifically reasonable,[1] and which is not present in committal to fire. Certainly committal to fire could be a powerful Christian symbol—of a dangerously one-sided doctrine of death and judgement, of that imbalance of theological emphasis which needs correction. There is no such symbolic imbalance in committal to earth or to water, for the destructive and judgemental aspect of death is as manifest in this as it is in committal to fire, and in a more appropriately natural and inevitable manner: at the same time the symbolism of future resurrection is also naturally present in committal to earth or to water, whereas it is not naturally present in committal to fire.

The straightforward simplicity of the symbolism of earth burial makes it theologically and liturgically the most appropriate form of committal. On the other hand, pastoral and sociological considerations are increasingly urged against it, and it is consequently becoming less and less common, even among practising Christians. Certainly there is nothing edifying about neglected graves in neglected churchyards, or row upon row of depressingly ugly monuments in depressingly vast and impersonal cemeteries; and in an overcrowded country the continued appropriation of large tracts of land for this purpose is clearly undesirable. Arguments based on these grounds, however, are not conclusive, because they are in fact arguments not against burial itself, but against the consequences of one particular form of it. And our current manner of burial is very little better, theologically and liturgically, than our current manner of cremation. For the point of committing the body to the earth is that the former should be absorbed by the latter as completely as possible: the symbolism of

[1] The death and resurrection symbolism in committal to the earth—the parallel with seed and grain and so forth—is sufficiently evident to need no further exposition here. It is equally present in committal to water, although both the mythology and the scientific facts which underlie it are less obvious and more complicated. Any reader who wishes to pursue the matter further should read Mircea Eliade's examination of it in his book *Patterns in Comparative Religion*.

committal to the earth requires this. But in current practice it is always delayed—and can, in certain circumstances, be largely, or even wholly, prevented—by the coffin; and it may also be symbolically contradicted by the custom of marking each individual grave by the erection of a more or less permanent monument.[1] Just as in cremation as it is currently practised, so in burial as it is currently practised: the essential theological and psychological symbolism of the committal is too often obscured. For just as committal to fire must *be* a committal to fire, so committal to earth must *be* a committal to earth—which means that the earth, like the fire, must be allowed to do its work of dissolution unhindered. It is not impossible today to design and make a cemetery in which *real* earth burial could be practised, without in any way departing from modern standards of hygiene and so forth. Such cemeteries would go a long way to solving the problem of land for burials, as any given plot could be re-used within a comparatively short space of time;[2] and because of this the reintroduction of the churchyard would be possible if and where it were desired. The propriety of churchyards and specifically Christian cemeteries is at present in debate among those theologians who are concerning themselves with these problems: personally I cannot see that any of our new theological insights tells against them—rather the contrary, indeed: and the churchyard or a cemetery close at hand

[1] Two distinct things are involved here—the natural reluctance to accept the fact of dissolution, and the natural desire to commemorate the departed. The first is theologically unjustifiable, and can be psychologically harmful, and it should be one of the pastoral objects of the compilers of a liturgy of committal to help people overcome it and attain a more realistic and more Christian attitude. The second, on the other hand, is positively desirable, both theologically and psychologically. It can be expressed, however, in a variety of ways, some of which are theologically justifiable and psychologically beneficial, while others are neither, and among the latter are those which enshrine reluctance to accept the fact of dissolution. Modern funerary monuments often fall into the latter category: the factors which combine to produce this effect are subtle and complex but their results can easily be perceived by comparing the aspect of a typical modern cemetery with that of a churchyard in the middle ages. The latter was theologically Christian and psychologically healthy: the former is neither.

[2] In the discussions which followed this and succeeding papers, it was pointed out that at least one London cemetery is so constituted geologically that any corpse buried in it—even in a coffin—is likely to be totally absorbed within ten years. It is evident that cemeteries of the kind proposed could be provided without disproportionate strain on scientific and financial resources.

is much to be preferred on practical grounds to the monster municipal cemetery at the back of beyond.[1]

Where there is a churchyard, of course, the committal procession presents no problem: where burial has to take place in a more or less distant cemetery, the processional material could be adapted in the way suggested for the journey to a crematorium. As for the actual committal itself, both the form of the ceremony and the accompanying words need profound rethinking, in order that it may not be an unworthy or inadequate climax to a liturgy of committal such as I have attempted to outline.

There remains the third possible form of disposal, committal to water, practical considerations in favour of which are suggested by Charles Brown in his paper.[2] As pointed out above,[3] there is an appropriate inherent symbolism in committal to water just as there is in committal to the earth. It is, however, a less effective symbolism, because it is less obvious and would require more explanation; and it is possible that there might be unfavourable psychological reactions to this form of committal. For this reason it does not seem that committal to water would be likely to prove a widely acceptable alternative to burial or cremation. But should committal to water become a viable alternative there need be no difficulty in creating an appropriate and effective ritual form of it.

There are important issues which have only been touched upon in passing and others which have not been considered at all: for example, the question of a liturgy of committal of the bodies of young children which presents an especially difficult pastoral problem for the liturgist to solve—theologically such a liturgy should be entirely joyful, whereas in fact the grief of the bereaved is likely to be greater than in almost any other situation.[4] A word must be added, however, on a problem mentioned earlier, the provision of suitable rites for the committal of the bodies of what can only be called semi-Christians. It is evident that a full Christian

[1] Some interesting thoughts on cemeteries will be found in Antonio Savioli "The Final Resting Place of Deceased Christians", and Theodor Filthaut, "Cemeteries and the Resurrection", in *Concilium*, loc. cit., pp. 27–33 and 33–7.

[2] p. 111.

[3] p. 81.

[4] In saying that such a liturgy should be entirely joyful I am of course taking for granted—which I should not necessarily assume in every context— the continuance of infant baptism.

liturgy of committal cannot appropriately be used over the body of one who, although he may have been baptized as an infant as a matter of social convention, has never in fact lived the Christian life, and has died as he has lived without any personal commitment to God in Christ. In the case of such a man—and he constitutes the majority of those whom the Church's ministers are called upon to commit today—a funeral liturgy replete with paschal triumph and eucharistic joy would be appropriate only in the correspondence of its tragic lack of meaning to that of his baptism at the other end of his life. The balance of joy and sorrow, hope and penitence has to be entirely reconsidered, and this means that a very different liturgy is called for, in structure as well as in content: in particular the eucharist, the very heart of the liturgy considered above, would hardly be appropriate.[1]

---

[1] A secondary but important problem, however, arises in this context—the assistance and consolation due to Christian mourners at such a funeral.

6

Architecture for Mourning

Peter B. Bond

I intend to consider in some detail the design of crematoria, but before doing so it will be useful to try to convey something of the underlying philosophy which has directed my inquiry, not only into this particular type of building, but into any problem confronting me concerning the nature and purpose of architecture.

The words used in the title "Architecture for Mourning" imply a connection between buildings and a state of feeling. It is the nature of this connection which forms the foundation of what I am trying to understand in architecture.

Architecture does not exist outside the context of our experience of it. This statement, though seemingly obvious, holds the key to much that needs to be understood and opens vast horizons to be explored. Architecture is not a thing apart but can provide a basis for a kind of communion between a series of spacial arrangements and the inner condition—or state—of an individual human being. It is our task to discover the processes of this communion. We must try to establish a basis on which we can recognize that certain patterns produce similar responses in most people. If we are able to do this there is a real possibility that the language of architecture will begin to be known again in the way I am sure it has been known in the past. It would provide a unity which is lacking in practically all aspects of life today.

To begin to understand this unity we have to search for something which is common to all men. Taking the simplest illustration, if any one of us received a blow from a hammer it would hurt;

if I received such a blow it would hurt me. From that moment on there would be unity between us concerning the nature of a blow from a hammer since it would relate to a direct and real experience. Divorced from the actual experience the concept "blow from a hammer" is meaningless.

Can this principle be extended to help our present inquiry? I think it can, and to elaborate on the example given let us imagine a completely flat desert with no landmark in sight. If one then adds to this scene one pole sticking up out of the ground, this pole, occupying a point in space, will become a focus of attention to which we are attracted in spite of ourselves.

Now imagine a second post appearing alongside the first. They would both still command our attention, but something else has been added. We should be able to walk between the two and therefore the element of direction has entered the situation. If we add further posts in pairs on the same axis as the first then each additional pair would further increase the strength of the direct-ional element thus created. The resulting corridor of posts would be a very compelling arrangement. If we were to place an object, perhaps a building, at the end of this corridor and were to approach the building down the length of this corridor we would all feel that we were approaching something of importance. By the time we had walked the whole way down the corridor our state would be such as to have elevated the building to something akin to sacred.

Take another example. If we have a room, perfectly plain and having a door at one end of it, we are able to walk into the room and feel its emptiness. If we then place a large object, such as a piece of sculpture, at the end of the room away from the door, then on entering our attention would immediately go towards the piece of sculpture. We would examine it in detail, thereby entering into a closer relationship with it. In this arrangement we will have created a quality of *silence*.

Now imagine that between the door end of the room and the object a perforated screen is erected which we are not permitted to penetrate. We may enter the room and stand in the space avail-able. We may observe the object through the perforated screen but we are no longer able to be intimate with it and are compelled to feel that the object is in its own special place. To the quality of silence would have been added a certain *sanctity* merely by the particular arrangement of the elements of and within the room.

You will notice that any question of a particular style of design does not enter into these illustrations. The responses they call forth are solely the result of spatial arrangements. Yet they do contain, I believe, an indication of experiences we would share, and therefore we could say that in these simple instances we could predict, with reasonable certainty, the responses likely to be experienced by most people who came across these particular arrangements.

One could develop illustrations of this kind until one had established a crude vocabulary to work with. This development would include examples of relative masses and how we feel ourselves drawn one way or another; the effect of volume in relation to the human being where we could recognize the effect, for instance, of walking in a narrow passage between two long and very high walls; or the reverse where we find ourselves in a vast room having a ceiling height of only ten feet. The examples would also bring out the effect on us of moving from one volume to another. The constriction felt when moving from a large volume to a small one and the feeling of broadening as we move from small to large. We would cover the effects of scale; the source of light, its quality, colour, and consequent effect on us.

However, this is an immense subject and could be discussed in itself, for many hours. For the present I hope it is sufficient to illustrate my belief that a common basis exists from which we could come to a real understanding of the part to be played by architecture, ceremony, and words in the subtle realm of human experience.

Having conveyed the broad factors which have to be taken into account we can now focus our attention more closely on the task of providing crematoria. The first question is what are these buildings for? This may appear to be a superfluous question, but it is my impression that there is more emphasis on the means of disposing of the mortal remains of the deceased person than on what the real role of these buildings should be, which is to provide a context in which the living can experience to the full the reality of death, and perhaps from this the privilege of life.

History has witnessed various forms of disposal, but each has been accompanied by ceremony. Ceremony, in its broadest sense, involves a series of movements, actions, and words which, together with the environment in which they take place, form a complete and significant pattern. A person experiencing this pattern should find in it a correspondence to the feelings which move him at the time. The degree to which this correspondence is achieved will determine the extent to which a person will be able to find expression of his feelings and the measure to which he is fulfilled. Something of this may be detected in the conclusions reached by Geoffrey Gorer who found that those mourners who were subjected to a more ritualistic form of mourning more readily adapted themselves to life after their bereavement. He quotes an American doctor who says: "Ceremonies have always been recognized as effective in the channelling or release or relaxation of the tensions to be dealt with in a crisis, quite apart from a belief in immortality."

If we feel that there is much greater benefit to be derived than at present it is necessary to realize the importance which must be attached to the task of providing these buildings and the ceremony which is to take place in them. For on those relatively rare times in a person's life when they come into contact with these buildings we are concerned by how they are impressed. Will their experience produce a deep and lasting recognition of the reality of death, not for the person who has died, but for themselves. What effect could this have on their lives? Further, what effect on the life of a society would result if all members of it carried with them this realization?

Lorens van der Post, in his book *Journey into Russia,* says something very relevant to this. Finding himself in the Ukraine, the scene of much fighting in the war, he asked his guide if he could be shown a military cemetery. His guide took him to a collective memorial. Van der Post explained that he was interested to see individual graves. The guide, looking rather perplexed, said she felt sure there must be such cemeteries in the Soviet Union, but she had never seen one. She then said that the monument they were in front of was for all the dead soldiers and surely it did not matter to the dead whether they were individually or collectively buried; once dead surely nothing mattered to the dead. Van der Post, commenting on this experience, says, "Perhaps it does not matter to the dead how they are disposed of, but I believe their treatment of the dead is a matter of great practical importance to the living. An important part of the way we live depends on our attitude to death and the dead, indeed I think the temptation to go to war could more readily be resisted in those peoples who break down the results of mass slaughter into its individual detail than in those who bulldoze the corpses into one vast impersonal grave. Communal graves do not haunt and warn the imagination so much as the vast reminders of single known and loved persons. The Unknown Warrior is impressive as a symbol, but the ghosts that pursue us are personal."

If there is any truth in the picture that emerges from what has been said up to now concerning the ceremony we are discussing, then it is clear the considerable responsibility we have in providing a context in which these subtle human experiences can find a place. This context, as I have tried to make clear, is not only the building we are to provide, not only the words of the service, nor again just the movement of the mourners themselves as the ceremony unfolds. The context is all of these things taken together and fused into a harmonious totality. Each aspect, large or small, reinforcing the main aim of the ceremony.

When I began studying these buildings it was the lack of this quality which disturbed me. They seemed to reflect little of what I felt was important about the event and I felt compelled to look closer into the problem and try to find a solution I could feel happier about.

I first looked into the history of the cremation movement in this country, and discovered a fact which I believe is very significant. The Cremation Society which started the movement in this country is a secular one. A group of far-seeing men, each distinguished in his own sphere, sensed the need, for a host of very relevant reasons, to revive the practice of cremation. At that time the Church was unsympathetic and the Establishment was shocked. Nevertheless, the movement continued and little by little the public came to see what the early pioneers had seen many years previously. The practice of cremation was not only unavoidable but many felt it to be desirable.

Many years after the movement began it was recognized by the Church but by that time the character of the practice was firmly established. We see, therefore, that the Church, which is the only corporate body concerned with the meaning and purpose of existence, was not responsible for laying down a liturgical pattern for these buildings in the way it has done in the churches it has

DD

built. Its role in the case of crematoria has been one of aquiescence in an already established practice. Cremation, in this country, is basically a secular arrangement to which religion has become attached. This is precisely the feeling these buildings impart and I believe this conflict between secular and religious is at the root of the failure of present-day crematoria. It is my view that this conflict can only be resolved on the basis of these experiences common to all men which I tried to touch on earlier.

Having looked, briefly, at the history of these buildings we must now look more closely into the existing plan of these buildings, and here it is necessary to try to understand precisely what factors disturb or what prevent the ceremony having the dignity it might. The form of these buildings does not derive from considerations of liturgy. This is not surprising since there is no rite for cremation. Yet for a great number of people cremation is a religious act, and it would be reasonable to expect the guiding principle, in those parts of the building used in a religious service, to be the liturgical expression of a religious rite. At the same time, since there are people who do not belong to the predominant religious group but to another, or perhaps to none at all, the building should deal with their needs separately and in a way which will cause no offence.

However, what happens in practice with present-day crematoria is that a group of people arrive and are confronted with a building of indifferent significance, often pompous rather than reverent, which they enter without ceremony. They sit whilst the minister conducts the service. At the words of committal various things can happen: a curtain can be drawn to cut off the coffin from the view of the mourners, or the coffin slowly descends through a hole in the floor, or it moves horizontally through an aperture in the wall. What has happened? The coffin has disappeared from view, that is all. It has passed into a room usually known as the "committal chamber", as shown in Diagram A, where it may be committed to the furnace immediately or it may not. We are able to see that the committal spoken of in the service is not a committal *at that time*, and as an event it is not integrated with the service. What is the significance of this fact for the mourners?

The committal is the reason for the existence of the building and the ceremony. It is the emotional climax of the ceremony. It is the moment of confrontation with the end of earthly life as we

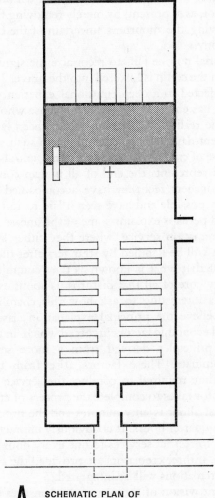

A SCHEMATIC PLAN OF
EXISTING CREMATORIA

(committal chamber shaded)

know it. It is my belief that this moment can only be expressed by a true and direct committal at that time and within a ceremonial context and not, as at present, by merely removing the coffin from view and leaving the mourners uncertain of the consummation of the ceremony.

In earth burial no one fails to recognize the significance of the moment when the coffin is lowered into the grave. Those witnessing it are subjected to a deep emotional experience and like all experiences it has entered into the life of those who stand around the grave. The reality of that moment has been faced, has been suffered. Present-day arrangements allow no such significance to exist in the case of crematoria. In earth burial, and also burial at sea, the committal represents the end of all human contact with the body. The mourners feel they have accompanied the corpse as far as humanly possible and have seen it laid to rest. This is very important and perhaps explains some of the unease felt by people attending a cremation service, where they either know or sense that the coffin will be handled by strangers after the service.

It is evident that what is known as the "committal chamber" lies at the very core of all that disturbs us about existing crematoria and it is interesting to ask how this chamber came into existence. I believe the principal explanation arises out of the functional and economic factors involved which, in the absence of any guiding principles derived from a more serious source, inevitably dominate. These factors arise from the difference between the time required to conduct the service and the time any one cremator takes to complete the process of cremation. The service will last about twenty minutes and the process of cremation one and a quarter hours. It is obviously impractical as well as uneconomical to restrict services to one every hour and a quarter and, therefore, if three cremators are provided the time cycles for services and cremations will be integrated.

Whilst the provision of three cremators ensures the economic use of the building it gives rise to the major problem of how to get the coffin to any one of the three cremators without destroying the singular character required. The obvious answer is the "committal chamber", but in achieving a solution to this entirely functional problem there has been introduced a void in place of a ceremonial moment of the utmost importance. Should this functional expedient be the main criterion governing the form of these buildings and the service taking place in them? Clearly this cannot be so and I determined to reject this formulation and to explore the possibility of achieving a true and direct committal to coincide with the words of the service and thereby integrating the ceremony with the act it celebrates.

In working on the problem I have attempted to give due significance to every aspect of the ceremony and to provide answers to the problems already mentioned in this talk. I should like to describe the results of this attempt, a plan of which is drawn in Diagram B (p. 94).

I have suggested that the mode of entry into the chapel should be in itself a ceremonial act. Two things are required to achieve this; time and distance; therefore, a ceremonial route leading from the hearse to the door of the chapel is required. The distance separating these two points will be determined by the need to allow a procession to form and move in concert, led by the minister, who will have walked down from the chapel to receive the mourners.

Assembly in the chapel is straightforward. The coffin is placed in a position of significance, related to the mourners and the minister, and prayer is conducted in the usual manner. Then the point of the service is reached where the committal is to take place, and what we are looking for is some ceremonial expressive of that moment. To bring out its full signficance the act must involve the minister, the coffin, and the mourners. At the same time it must solve the problem of getting the coffin to a place where one of the cremators is located. Since access to the cremators is no longer from the chapel itself, the whole assembly must move out of the chapel. This seems to me to be a most important idea, since the act of prayer differs very considerably in character from the act of committal and their juxtaposition in existing crematoria detracts from both, and, I believe, gives rise to the shock that many people feel.

Removing the committal to a place outside the chapel leaves the chapel solely as a place of prayer, and by the absence of the device used for removing the coffin there is nothing to distract the mourners as they pray.

To preserve the individual and private aspect of the ceremony for each of the services, there should be three separate places to which an assembly can move. There are other important advantages

PLAN OF SUGGESTED ARRANGEMENT OF CREMATORIA

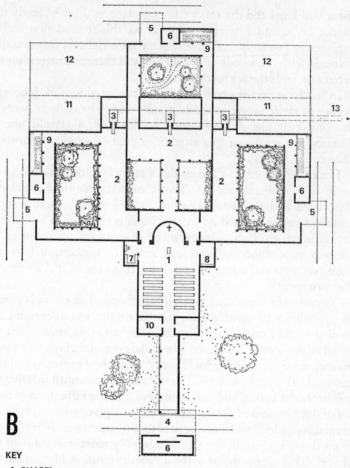

B

KEY

1 CHAPEL
2 COMMITTAL COURT
3 CREMATORS
4 ENTRANCE FOR CHRISTIAN CEREMONIES
5 EXITS (AND ENTRANCES FOR NON-CHRISTIAN CEREMONIES)
6 WAITING AND LAVATORIES
7 CHOIR AND ORGAN
8 RETIRING ROOM FOR BEARERS
9 VERTICAL FLOWER DISPLAY
10 VESTRY
11 SERVICE ROOM
12 YARD
13 DUCT TO REMOTE FLUE

offered by having three spaces. Once an assembly has moved
from the chapel to the place of committal, the mourners have at
their disposal any period of time up to seventy-five minutes from
the time of their arrival at the crematorium chapel. This period
can never be less and eliminates the possibility of mourners being
hurried through the service due to demands being made on the
crematorium. It also allows for the possibility of the communal
act of talking together both before and after the service, which
some people feel to be desirable. The chapel would also be freed
for perhaps ten minutes or a quarter of an hour before the
following service is due. This allows any special arrangements to
be made at leisure. At busy times the early or late arrival of a
cortège would cause no embarrassment since a total margin of
about twenty minutes has been achieved, due to the fact that for a
service lasting about twenty-five minutes in all only ten minutes or
a quarter of an hour is spent in the chapel itself.

The three separate places which, in turn, the groups of
mourners move to obviously need to be enclosed by walls and the
assembly must also be provided with cover. These requirements
are answered by the cloistered courts I show on my plan.

The movement of the mourners to these courts also serves
another purpose I feel to be very important. By passing out of the
chapel into the open air and meeting the small level of background
noise; by coming into contact with a court landscaped with plants,
trees, and pools with perhaps running water, the mourners are
subjected to an environmental change which will allow them to
recover from the inner quiet of prayer and to brace themselves
for the actual committal itself. This is, of course, exactly what
happens in earth burial.

The most significant feature in this arrangement of the building
is that the actual committal is no longer carried out by municipal
operatives but by the minister himself, who will start the movement of the coffin as he utters the words of committal. This
movement of the coffin will continue until the coffin is actually
inside the cremator and the minister's hand will be the last to
touch the coffin. Thus the committal is direct and true to the words
of the service, with nothing coming between the ceremony and its
fulfilment.

On the question as to whether or not the mourners should see
the coffin entering the flames, views differ so violently that I

considered an alternative necessary. The plan shows a "baffle chamber" which allows the doors of the aperture in the court to close before those into the cremator itself open to receive the coffin. If desired both can open simultaneously, and so permit a view of the coffin entering the flames. In this way the mourners may satisfy their wishes on this question, still within a ceremonial context which they are not provided with at present. It also allows for any changes in attitude which may develop in relation to witnessing the coffin entering the flames.

It is worth noting that owing to the impossibility of permitting the noise of the cremator jets to invade the essential quiet of the chapel, the evolution of the act of committal has hitherto been restricted. With the introduction of committal courts there opens up the possibility that the committal could become an act of great dignity in which the mourners would participate more fully.

There remains the problem of the need for a physical link between the cremator chambers in order to provide access for the staff who have to operate the controls. In order that each court can be accessible from the chapel, and the mourners can leave each court separately, the link between the cremator chambers needs to be below or above ground level, and I have suggested this link should be below ground to preserve the separateness of each of the courts.

The road system around the buildings, illustrated in Diagram C (p. 97), is a simple matter which to a large extent eliminates the possibility of one cortège meeting another, as long as there are two site entrances and the necessary administration arranged.

Here, then, we have a building in which the religious rite can be given the fullest ceremonial expression called for, and yet avoids the current dilemma of people attending crematoria who have no desire for a religious service, but do feel the need for some dignified ceremonial. At present they are compelled to use the chapel as a place of assembly, and a number of embarrassing devices have been evolved whereby crucifixes can be hidden or taken away or, at worst, submitted to. In the arrangement I suggest such people may come to the committal court directly without passing through the chapel. They can enter, move on a ceremonial route to the point at which committal takes place, and retire on a ceremonial route to their waiting cars.

In describing this suggestion for the form of crematoria it has

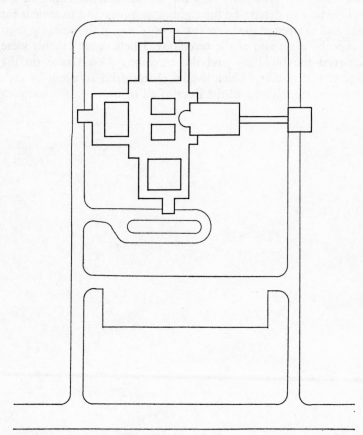

C ROAD SYSTEM

been possible here to deal only with the plan, but one hopes that the broad structural sequence proposed for the ceremony has been made clear. In clarifying each stage of the ceremony there now exists the possibility of using all our understanding of the architecture to determine the right atmosphere and treatment for each and to attempt to ensure that every detail of the building reinforces the main aim of the ceremony. I believe that if this were achieved the buildings and the ceremony would take on the dignity and nobility which should characterize an event of such profound significance in the lives of all of us.

7

The Environment of Disposal
THE INTERIOR

Gilbert Cope

The purpose of this chapter is to discuss the architectural setting, the furnishing, and the interior décor of the "point of departure" or "place of ritual farewell" at which the deceased is removed from the bereaved. Using the analogy of a journey, the reference is to the "waiting-room" of a railway-station or a port rather than the platform, the dockside, or the airstrip—i.e., the "chapel" or "committal-room" rather than the graveside or the furnace-room.

The considerable variation in funeral customs within one faith makes it difficult to avoid some overlapping of topics in the discussion, and further complications arise when the fact is taken into account that the funeral rites of several quite different religions may have to be conducted in the same room. Thus, while the discussion will be mainly concerned with the public liturgical environment for nominally Christian commital, i.e., the chapel of a cemetery or crematorium, some consideration has to be given to the previous lodgement of the coffin either at home, in a church, in a hospital mortuary, or in a funeral director's "chapel of repose".

Again, there are several different points at which the ceremonies may actually finish for all, or some, of those concerned, e.g., the home, the church, one of the "chapels", or at the open earth-grave, or the incinerator.

The matter is complex and will be discussed under the headings: Doctrine; History; Psychology and Aesthetics; Liturgy and Logistics.

DOCTRINE

The environment of disposal in its architectural quality and its interior decoration can reflect something of the attitude of the mourners towards death, and it can express some aspect of their beliefs, hopes, and fears, and their expectations concerning a "life after death". The traditional concepts of "resurrection" and "immortality" are still the subject of learned theological debate, though they are not now a central matter of concern; today's religious dialogues are focused rather upon the role of the Church in the world and the sacred-secular relationship. Few Christians would wish to commit themselves to anything like a precise forecast concerning post-mortal existence, and most are content to speak in general terms about "the survival of a recognizable personality" or "living at a new level in the dimension of eternity". But, although they would generally regard the mortal remains of the deceased as theologically without significance (i.e., by rejecting a literal interpretation of "the resurrection of the body"), they would wish the corpse to be treated with reverence and the ashes to be disposed of in a respectful manner. This attitude would seem to have much more to do with regard for the past life of the deceased person, and the mystery of life in general, than with any particular view of possible persistence of individual personality such as might be expressed in a doctrine of the "immortality of the soul" or the "company of saints with the risen Lord in heaven".

Again, assuming that there may be some kind of survival of recognizable personality, most Christians would prefer to remain "agnostic" concerning both the immediate and the ultimate destiny of whatever may survive and persist. Medieval speculation elaborated from biblical sources a grandiose scheme of Purgatory, Judgement, Hell, and Heaven; early Protestantism generally reverted to the stark alternatives of Hell or Heaven and paid scant attention to the role of angels, demons, and saints; contemporary belief at the academic level is non-committal (if the term is not inappropriate), while at the "popular" level it seems to be supposed that the soul of the departed is immediately received into the divine presence without more ado. The *In Memoriam* notices in local newspapers are a remarkable testimony to popular beliefs about death and heaven, and the following example is quite typical:

* * * Loving birthday memories of our dear mom 76 today. No flowers or cards, but dear God take this message to our mom above. Tell her how we miss her and give her our love. Put your arms around her, give her all your care, for that angel was our mom, the best beyond compare.

The apparent contradiction between salvation through the death of Christ and the prospect of the Last Judgement, with the possibility of a sentence of suffering in Hell, has long constituted something of a doctrinal dilemma for Christians. This puzzle is now solved intellectually by denying the spatial and temporal characteristics previously ascribed to Heaven and Hell, while, from the popular mind Hell has disappeared and with it the need for a Last Judgement. In other words, the mythological geography and the calendar of events of the "next world" have been abandoned in favour of speculative pattern of human-divine relationships. At the intellectual level, the interaction of Hebrew eschatology and Greek metaphysics in the past produced a Christian synthesis of somewhat precarious character, and this has now become so abstract that it is difficult to visualize at all.

In terms of environmental décor, this means that very little of the traditional pictorial imagery and symbolic iconography of death may still be used meaningfully. Thus, Stanley Spencer's quasi-naturalistic paintings of the Day of Resurrection as it might be at Gallipoli or at Cookham produce a curious sense of embarrassment, and any attempt now to depict the Last Judgement and the fate of the departed in Heaven or Hell would be out of tune with the ill-defined aspirations of believers.

While it is easy to judge what is iconographically unacceptable today, it is not so easy to suggest how modern artists might be commissioned to assist in the creation of an environment of disposal which would express current abstract hopes, and, at the same time, minister to the comfort of the bereaved. Positive suggestions will be better made after a brief historical survey of how Christians have decorated their funerary "waiting-rooms" in the past. Thus may the way be prepared for the necessary dialogue of the future.

HISTORY

We are exceptionally well informed concerning the character of early Christian funerary art because of the survival of pre-Constantinian burial places—the catacombs. Many symbolic hieroglyphs, figures, and scenes are to be found in the fresco paintings which adorn the walls of these underground rooms and passages, but the main emphases are upon *prayer* and *deliverance*. There are numerous examples of a standing figure with arms outstretched in prayer—expressive of confident hope and joy in spite of the sorrow of bereavement.

However, the major concern is to express the conviction that Christ delivers from disease and death, and that through identification with him the deceased will achieve salvation and liberation. The subjects chosen to illustrate this theme are mainly of two kinds —"typological" figures or occasions from the Old Testament or Apocrypha, and "healing" miracles from the New Testament. Thus, a favourite four-scene sequence is the story of Jonah— thrown overboard, swallowed by the sea-monster, regurgitated, lying at naked ease in Paradise—a "type" of death and resurrection referred to by Jesus himself (Matt. 12.40). Other similar scenes include Noah in the ark, Daniel in the lions' den, and the three men in the fiery furnace—all suggest salvation from death by divine intervention.

Secondly, deliverance from the disease of mortality and the paralysis of death is expressed in representations of the gospel healings of various people and especially in the raising of Lazarus from the dead. A further New Testament reference to a future hope is to be seen in the imagery of a eucharistic meal: not only is this a representation of the Last Supper and of the contemporary "requiem mass" and "funeral meal" (or *agape*): it is also a symbol of the banquet of the Messiah in which living and departed would join when Christ came in power. The worshippers were reminded by this sign of St Paul's words that participation in the eucharist was a "showing forth of the Lord's death till he come" (1 Cor. 11.26), and, thus, in the context of death an expression of the hope of resurrection. This particular symbol of the *corporate* character of the post-mortal hope maintained a very important aspect of the original Christian expectation and one which tends to be overlooked as pictorial and sculptured memorials to *individual* persons come to replace the social symbols.

The rest of the history of funerary art in Christendom is really a sequence of fashions in sculpture and literary style of the comparatively well-to-do—starting from the self-commemorating sarcophagi of Roman citizens. We are all familiar with the tombs of the medieval nobility and the Renaissance gentry; we may be fascinated by the baroque memorials and flamboyant inscriptions of wealthy landowners and merchants in the eighteenth and nineteenth centuries and also with the more modest memorials in the country churchyards. Further, we know something (perhaps too much) of the mass-produced images and inscriptions of this century's cemeteries and crematoria.

The memorials within a church obviously form part of the interior environment if part of the funeral ceremony is conducted there but, equally obviously, neither in chapels of rest nor in cemetery and crematorium chapels do these former tributes to the departed provide an element in the décor. The installation within churches and chapels of memorials is nowadays either discouraged altogether or limited to very simple wall-plaques. In other words, recollection of the previously deceased is not visually encouraged. All that seems to be aimed at is an indeterminate atmosphere of undoubted hygiene and vague uplift, and I wonder if the reintroduction of some visually recognizable and traditional symbols might not be advantageous in encouraging the reasonable expression of grief rather than its suppression.

PSYCHOLOGY AND AESTHETICS

It is natural that the main focus of attention should really be the corpse, but it is also natural to adopt various ways of "veiling" the actuality of the dead body. Thus, the body is cleansed and made to look more or less lifelike; it is clothed in some fashion; it is covered by a pall or encased in a box; the coffin itself may be covered by a pall and flowers and other tokens of reminiscence and respect. In brief, in the environment of disposal the mourners no longer see the corpse at all. It is all the more important, therefore, that they should see "what happens" to the decorated container. At least, it is my opinion that in the process of bereavement it is psychologically desirable for most people that the "departed" should not only depart but should be seen to depart ceremonially, and not mysteriously disappear—down a hole or through a wall or behind a curtain—to the sound of indeterminate music and incomprehensible utterance. To my mind such practices are not only psychologically profoundly unsatisfactory for the bereaved, but offensive alike to believers, non-believers, and the great mass of those in between. Rather than such a disturbing and inconclusive disappearance it would be better simply to leave the coffin where it is when the mourners go out of the chapel.

In the case of earth-burial, crude though it may be, some of the uncertainty is avoided: even the plastic grass cannot disguise the fact that this is the final action on earth. Now, it may well be that for some people such finality of ceremony is better avoided (and I think that this is a subject deserving of much more study than it appears to get), but I am convinced that greater clarity of liturgy and ceremony in a crematorium chapel is much to be desired. There is much to be said for the *option* of actually seeing the committal to the flames being offered to those who are so advised; (an analogy is the husband's option to be present at the birth of his child). One imagines that few of the Christian faith would take up this option, nor do I think it should be encouraged generally, and this is all the more reason, I suggest, for making the removal of the deceased from the chapel unambiguous.

Because the corpse is the unavoidable focus of attention at some stage in the whole process of disposal, and because this is a harrowing fact, it is also important to provide an *alternative* focus of attention for the mourners. By this I do not mean a *substitute* focus so that they may be encouraged to "forget" the real focus, but an additional focal point which is also the "opposite pole" of grief, namely, hope and joy.

This consideration applies to all kinds of "chapels of repose and departure"—whether they be in churches, in funeral directors' premises, or in cemeteries and crematoria. Every one of these places is to some extent a "funerary oratory"—a place where prayers (or their non-religious equivalent) are offered in the presence of the corpse. It would, therefore, seem to be desirable to have some alternative visual focus—and, indeed, this is usually supplied in the form of a plain cross and a covered table which looks like a nineteenth-century altar but which is very seldom, if ever, used for the celebration of the eucharist. Personally, I find a counterfeit altar a most repugnant symbol; nor do I like those catafalques which are deliberately made to resemble altars. To have an element of dissimulation at the heart of this ceremony is surely to be avoided at all costs, even if popular vaguely religious associations with a conventional genuine Christian altar still

persist. The positive reasons why such associations survive would
be an interesting question to investigate, but one of the negative
reasons is undoubtedly the absence of any obvious alternative;
and, thus, we are brought back to the problem of imagery.

If the traditional symbols have lost their immediate impact, and
if more or less naturalistic imaginative scenes of Heaven and Hell
are unacceptable, what is to be done?

There can, I think, be no "instant funerary art", but I do think
that some of the *semi-abstract* idioms of much modern art are
eminently suitable for the provision of the secondary focus. For
Christian mourners, the eyes need to be able to rest upon a symbol
or figure which is neither an "illustration" nor a completely non-
figurative invention, but rather a composition which has some
recognizable associations with religious hope. Similarly, believers
of other faiths will have their own signs and symbols susceptible
of this kind of treatment. Pictures, embroidered hangings,
sculpture, and so forth which are evocative without being
obtrusive are what I have in mind. Works of art are needed which
do not draw all attention away from the corpse and catafalque nor
from the liturgical action and the disposal ceremony, but which
yet provide an alternative focus for intercession and meditation.

Such objects would naturally help to establish the "mood" of
the chapel—the atmosphere of bitter-sweet departure. Ideally, of
course, they would form an integral part of a chapel architecture
positively designed to create the desired "atmosphere". Opinions
will vary concerning what atmosphere is most to be desired, and
a work of art possessing quality is bound to arouse strong feelings.
Nevertheless, I hope that those concerned with the interior décor
of funerary chapels will give serious thought to commissioning
artists for a focal work of this kind.

An example which springs to my mind is Ceri Richards'
"Supper at Emmaus" (which hangs behind the altar in the Oxford
college chapel of St Edmund Hall). This painting in no sense
represents "what it looked like at the time", but it is quickly
recognizable for what it is—a fellowship meal which bridges the
gap between the living and the dead—a communion which spans
the centuries from the time of Christ until today. Although many
people might not "like" the painting overmuch—the figures do
not conform to current cinephotography in the biblical epics—
yet there is clearly presented a situation with which most people

could "identify" easily enough—a friendly meal in which Jesus is known in the breaking of the bread.

I believe that it is in such directions that an answer will be found to the problem of creating a funerary environment which is at once expressive of religious faith, not lacking in integrity, positively therapeutic for those who mourn, stimulative of sincere prayer, and satisfying to those of artistic sensitivity.

LITURGY AND LOGISTICS

The total interior environment of disposal cannot be considered only in terms of theological symbolism and psychological response: important practical questions of "time and motion" also have to be studied. The coffin has to be brought somehow from outside to inside; the minister must liturgically "conduct" this procession with more or less ceremony; the bearers and the mourners must get themselves from their transport to their places in the chapel; the coffin must rest upon something and must be ceremonially removed (unless it is allowed to remain in the same place until the mourners have left); all present must remove themselves, either to the graveside or directly back to their transport (though possibly some may go to the place of incineration). A Christian funeral service may take fifteen to twenty minutes in chapel or church; the visit to the grave or the cremator may take roughly the same time, but cremation itself takes over an hour and may not be begun immediately after the end of the service. Another funeral party may well have just left the chapel and yet another may be waiting at the door.

Clearly, entrances, gangways, and exits are important, not to mention the various mechanical devices which may be employed to move the coffin from one place to another. All these considerations are bound to affect the "feeling" of the chapel, and at a very busy cemetery or crematorium there is a positive danger that the "waiting-room" may seem rather like a corridor.

Other contributions to this book deal in detail with the questions of liturgical movement and architectural layout and here it is possible merely to mention the need to remember the possible aesthetic side-effects of purely utilitarian solutions to the logistic problems. Again, some provision often has to be made for the rapid conversion of a Christian chapel into a serviceable and acceptable room for the performance of the final *rites de passage* customary in other faiths. Obviously, some compromises have to be made until the number of funerals in any of the non-Christian religions justifies the provision of a separate chapel for that faith.

However, the interior "atmosphere" of any volume is only partly established by its size, its entrances and exits, and its furnishings—practical and symbolic. Equally determinative of how people feel when they are inside are the proportions, the forms, the acoustics, the colours, the textures, and above all the intensity and the distribution of the light. These factors are all, in principle, controllable, and a skilful architect-designer can create whatever "atmosphere" his client requests. And so we are back with the question concerning what kind of interior atmospheric effect best accords with the prevailing mood of the mourners and best expresses their religious hope. This is bound to be largely a matter of opinion and individual temperament, but it is hoped that this rather inconclusive discussion will, nevertheless, be a useful contribution to a dialogue which must continue.

The Environment of Disposal
THE EXTERIOR

Charles Brown

The environment of disposal reflects our attitudes to death and the dead; it must also accommodate the practical problems which arise in the disposal of corpses.

Our attitudes to the dead can be loosely classified under four headings—fear, reverence, honour, and love. First, *fear*. In our attitudes to death rationally incompatible beliefs easily coexist, and pre-logical feelings stubbornly survive in advanced civilizations. The aboriginal fears of primitive man survive in some primitive rituals which continue to be practised. When we close the mouth and eyes of the dead and arrange them in an attitude of peaceful repose we do so in the belief of performing an act of piety, but there is reason to suppose that in these acts there is a residue of the measures taken against the dead in order to prevent them from harming the living. Such ancient and horrible measures as putting out their eyes, tying or even mutilating their hands and feet, sealing them up in hollow trees—all these stem from a fear of the deceased. This fear also stems from an inability to understand how something living has ceased to live, and from lack of knowledge there always arises fear. Man finds it difficult to believe that the extinction of life means the end of human existence. "To what base uses we may return, Horatio! Why may not imagination trace the noble dust of Alexander till he find it stopping a bung-hole. Imperial Caesar dead and turned to clay, might stop a hole to keep the wind away." Thus Hamlet mused in the graveyard. But belief in continued existence itself sometimes leads to fear, and hence the attempt to render the dead powerless. Alternatively, attempts may be made to make the dead happy: for instance, in ancient Egypt the dead were often represented with open eyes and open mouth so that they could continue to consume the food left with them.

Secondly, *reverence*. It is instinctive that man should wish to honour what he has valued, and the remains of a respected person are not just spurned when life is extinct. Reverence for the dead has led to the practice of "seemly funerals" and "decent burials", and the reverence can even lead to worship as in the cult of the martyrs.

Thirdly, *honour*. Honour is akin to reverence but is perhaps manifested more in physical terms. The body may have gone but it can be honoured by representation in material terms or in eulogies of the virtues of the dead. Often honour of the dead has led to provision of something for the living; for example, in medieval times this could take the form of a splendid effigy, and even a church to contain the effigy.

Fourthly, *love*. The very human sentiment of affection complicates our attitude, and this sentiment is most to the fore today. Human bonds of affection are severed by death, and often it is sought through material form to continue to express that love by the provision of some physical symbol.

Such attitudes to the dead—fear, reverence, honour, love—can be seen manifested in the physical environment of our places of disposal. The past has seen many methods of disposal. It has seen the practice of disposal by exposure, incineration, refrigeration, embalming, water and ship burial, and even by cannibalism! But by far the most common practice is that of inhumation—burial in the ground. The preparation of a grave is motivated by a desire to make a safe place for the body. In earliest times the object was to preserve it from disturbance or destruction, or even to provide a home for the spirit as a residence rather than a receptacle. The grave is a place where the deceased can be visited and whence they may still exert an influence over their survivors. This attitude is passing today, but nuances remain. Our own attitudes in the West have developed from the pyramids of Egypt to the flat grave slab and, until recently, the most commonly accepted form of burial has been interment in the ground. "Dust to dust", in the context of a civilization based largely upon Christianity, has seemed to be the most fitting means of disposal of the dead.

Present practices inevitably reflect former customs, but, with the increasing population of the world and a natural acceptance of the health hazard of the decaying human body, it has become increasingly common to advocate cremation. Many people have found it difficult to accept this artificial hastening of natural processes. We accept the graveyard, the decent burial within the ground, the natural process of decay, the grand tombs of the past, the simple mounds, the weathered gravestones, the sense of beauty, peace, and repose; but the violent act of cremation has been found repugnant. Some have found it difficult to balance this seemingly unnatural act with a reverence, love, and respect for the personality which formerly resided in the decaying body. To others, however, cremation seems more desirable than slow dissolution in the ground, and so the prejudice is gradually disappearing. However, even cremation still leaves a residue and so the problem of disposal is greatly reduced but not entirely eliminated.

What alternatives are there for disposal of the physical remains? First, burial in churches. This is now most unusual. It was always reserved for the great and is now accorded only to the very great indeed, or to the very influential! Today most of our ancient churches are fully occupied below ground level, and our present laws of hygiene and health do not encourage burial within a new building. Secondly, burial in churchyards. This may still be possible in a small country parish, and nothing could be more proper than that a believer should be buried near the place where he worshipped in life and that his earthly residue should remain near the community where he was loved. Unfortunately, many churchyards are now closed and thus the great majority of burials take place in private or local authority cemeteries. Such cemeteries are usually situated away from the centre of life of a community, formerly on the outskirts but now, perhaps, enveloped by surburban housing. Many of these graveyards were established in the last century and are a memorial of the taste of that century. (Burial in private ground is lawful provided it is sanctioned by the Public Health authorities—for instance, David Lloyd George was buried in a private place of his own choice—but this practice is also something reserved for the wealthy and influential.)

Disposal in the sea has long been practised and is not unknown today. It is surprising that the sea, used for every other waste disposal, is not used more for the disposal of our dead. Cremation, followed by grinding the residue, obviously has a great advantage, in that it reduces the bulk of the body to a very small amount of ash. This ash contained in an urn can be buried in the ordinary ways and, further, burial of ashes can take place in churches or closed churchyards. In fact, burial of ashes can be in one's own garden, or the sea, or in any place, for they are not a health hazard. Further, ashes may be scattered over ground where they are quickly assimilated and disappear. But even such scattering can be a problem when ashes are scattered over the same spot for some time: "concretion" (a cementing of the ashes together into a hard lump) must be avoided, and insertion of the ashes into a small hole can eliminate this problem.

Such then are methods of disposal, and now some account must be given of the environment. In the medieval age the parish graveyard was merely a grassed enclosure dominated by a free standing cross, where individual marking of the graves was probably not customary at all, and from which periodically all the bones were removed and stored in a charnel house. In later times, inscribed stones marked the place of burial, and the virtues and merits of the life of wealthy individuals were often commemorated. Tombs of table form provided ample surface for inscriptions or tablets on the church wall near to the place of burial were inscribed. For lesser mortals marking the grave eventually became common. Fortunately this practice coincided with a period of general good taste, and thus we are left with many beautiful environments created in the eighteenth century in our churchyards. The nineteenth century with its expansion of population, its general lowering of taste, its sacrifice of the craftsmen to the factory, and the slowly increasing wealth amongst the whole population led to the establishment of large cemeteries and the individual memorials commemorating in rather more sentimental fashion the life of the deceased and the hope of that person for the future. These crowded bone-and-stone yards can now be seen in every part of the country, and the harshness of the materials is now alleviated a little by weathering and softened even more by neglect; crosses, prevalent as a result of the Tractarian Movement, now lean crazily in many directions, but trees have now grown mercifully to hide the worst taste and even give a quiet dignity to these marble collections as crowded as any Victorian chimneypiece. Now are manifested other all too human factors—pride and propriety, and even guilt. These are factors totally concerned with the living—with what one's neighbour may think of the degree to which one commemorates the departed, whether the size of the memorial will in some way reflect one's affection for the departed or one's own wealth. "Keeping up (or rather down) with the Joneses" was very much apparent in Victorian times and is still distressingly so in our own. Some degree of control has been exercised in churchyards where the incumbent has the power of approval and the worst excesses are avoided, but in the average local authority cemetery they are often seen. Even there the problems of maintenance are more difficult to solve now that labour is not so plentiful. The twentieth-century lavish memorials are more distasteful than those of the nineteenth century, for the latter were backed by a more sure and convinced Christian faith. Now a memorial is described in the catalogues as "a tribute", and one finds designs described in such terms as "Framed in the arch-ways of memories a little angel drops a flower and a tear, and the canopy is richly embellished with carved ivy leaf and provides space for the engraving of the family name," or "We believe this monument to be an achievement in memorial art. The cross and roses carved on the headrock, together with the spacious inscription tablet, form a headstone of special merit. Roses, a symbol of love and affection, are repeated in a similar setting on the footpost (if ivy-leaf, lily or tulip carving is preferred in place of roses this should be stated when ordering)." It is not stated of what these other plants are symbols!

In many places attempts are made to be rid of these excesses by forbidding the kerbs and insisting on headstones only. Aesthetically and for practical reasons of maintenance this is a much more desirable factor, for what is more dead than the physical expression of a memory forgotten? Adjoining sections of a churchyard can show how quickly the dead are forgotten. Those who originally cherished the memory may not have died themselves but have merely moved to another area. Sadness is increased for those at an interment if they glance around and see what twenty years will do to a memory. Bright green marble chippings or plastic flowers do little more to alleviate the sense that remembrance itself is dying than does the physical neglect of a grave. Much can be learned from the simple dignity of war cemeteries where the uniformity of the headstones stresses the uniformity of our human nature: there is certainly created a quiet, rhythmical, and peaceful environment where the senses are not aesthetically shocked by vagaries of taste or the evidences of human neglect. At another extreme, a very telling symbol is constituted by a plain lawn with no visible stones, dominated by a single cross or other emblem, and having only simple marking tablets and the usual complement of flowers.

Turning to cremation, as has been mentioned above, the burial of the ashes in the container can take place occasionally in churches, and often in enclosed churchyards. This is an example of how the remains of believers can be interred symbolically near their place of worship; here simple flat stones can be easily maintained, and, though individual in character, may enhance rather than detract from the appearance of the graveyard. More often than not, however, the ashes are not interred in an urn but are scattered. Again this can be done in a selected area of a closed churchyard. There is also the practice of placing the urns in an arcaded columbarium and applying a commemorative tablet. Here an atmosphere of peaceful dignity is easily achieved, but there are obvious space limitations. By far the most common method for the disposal of ashes is scattering in a garden of remembrance adjacent to a crematorium, and usually the name of the deceased is inscribed in a book of remembrance contained in an enclosure overlooking the garden. Plants or trees within the garden can sometimes be inscribed for a certain period as a memorial to the departed, but this is sensibly regarded as something which possibly after ten or fifteen years will not be renewed and, thus, the same or a new tree will be dedicated to another person. It is surprising that a large open space is so often found dedicated to the garden of rest, for peace and repose are not often induced by the atmosphere created by this type of landscaping. It is seldom found that the buildings within a cemetery are planned to blend into the landscape of the cemetery. The chapel is frequently an effete version of the traditional church set in its churchyard, with the cremator flues ineffectually disguised as a bell tower. Even modern examples in this country show little integration of the building with the environment. The building complex should be an enclosure within, not apart from, the cemetery or garden of rest, and it should have the same characteristics as the surrounding landscape into which it must be integrated. And the landscape itself must be carefully formed. Insubstantial flowering trees, large expanses of lawn and innumerable rose beds reflect a superficial attitude, whereas the deeply developed Victorian churchyard or cemetery has now in its maturity captured a more appropriate atmosphere. In continental Europe some of the most satisfying environments of disposal are to be found within an area of established trees. The light confines of a coppice, for example, may awaken a primeval sense of natural protection—both of the remains of the dead and for those who visit such a place of burial or scattering.

What then should guide our attitude to the external environment for disposal of the dead? We must give the subject open consideration, for our present lack of consideration is characteristic of our present silent embarrassment. Places of disposal have not been given the careful thought that has been given to other aspects of our physical environment—to our houses, our urban developments, our national parks, and our conservation areas.

A comparable approach to the environment of disposal would embody a sense of respect, love, and affection for things past and a desire to preserve these qualities for the future: to express, in fact, the permanence of the qualities which do outlive the body. Is it possible to express such qualities materially? Only nature by its annual renewal of plant growth seems to be symbolic of the hoped-for resurrection, and it is with *planting* that the environment of disposal should be largely formed. The ancient practice of taking flowers to the tomb is a reflection of this proper attitude, but careful planning is necessary to ensure that these tributes are integrated into the environment and do not form an untidy addition to it.

The desire to commemorate will probably continue and, therefore, present controls must be strengthened if our cemeteries are not to be as untidy as neglected mason's yards. Perhaps all but the simple headstone or flagstone must be prohibited? Perhaps an unmarked grave and a book of remembrance is all that will be allowed? We cherish and have learnt much from the gravestones and memorials of the past, but in this crowded world we must look for a neater and more compact means of commemoration.

How can the essential improvements be achieved? Would it not be better to separate cemetery and crematorium? Perhaps cremation facilities might eventually be incorporated into some places of everyday worship, though this would certainly not be acceptable today. Techniques of cremation are improving and the desired objective of complete combustion would obviate a second act of disposal and then commemoration alone would have to be taken into account.

Our immediate task is clear: to encourage public and open discussion of the problem. In this process the Church should have an important part to play. Such discussion will not rapidly change the delicate, mysterious, highly personal, and emotionally charged attitude of man to death, but it may do much to improve and provide a fitting environment of disposal.

APPENDIX

1. The cremation of a human body is a highly emotional occasion for many of those taking part in the service. This should never be forgotten by the officials of the Crematorium, who should combine to create and maintain an atmosphere of reverence and respect throughout the entire proceedings.

2. The funeral director shall observe the regulations drawn up by the Cremation Authority. He is responsible for the provision of sufficient bearers to convey the coffin reverently from the hearse to the catafalque. When the coffin is in position on the catafalque or deposited in the rest room or Chapel of Repose at the Crematorium his responsibility towards it ceases, and that of the Cremation Authority begins.

3. No official of a Cremation Authority shall conduct the business of a funeral director.

4. A body shall not be removed from the Crematorium after the Service of Committal.

5. No portion of the coffin or its contents shall be removed following the Committal Service; they shall be put into the cremator exactly as they are received on the catafalque.

6. Once a coffin, with its contents, has been placed in the cremator, it shall not be touched or interfered with until the process of incineration is completed.

7. No person shall be permitted to enter the committal room without the express permission of the superintendent. In cases where the representatives of the deceased express the desire to witness the placing of the coffin in the cremator, the superintendent shall give permission to two representatives to enter for this purpose.

8. Each body, whether adult or child, given to the care of the Cremation Authority shall be cremated separately. An exception shall be

permitted in appropriate cases where mother and baby may be cremated in the same coffin provided the necessary Authority to Cremate has been granted in both cases.

9. It frequently occurs that ornaments and rings, or dentures, of gold and other precious metals, are present on the body brought for cremation. In the process of Cremation these metals are not destroyed, but are present, in dull, misshapen form among the ashes. Care should be taken to separate such metals from the ashes, and a receptacle should be provided in which they should be retained for subsequent disposal in accordance with the directions of the Cremation Authority, or higher Authority.

10. The utmost care shall be taken to ensure that the ashes resulting from each cremation shall be kept separate. Following their removal from the cremator, the ashes shall be reduced and placed in separate containers whilst awaiting final disposal. If the ashes are to be scattered on the Garden of Rest, the ceremony shall be conducted with the greatest reverence and respect. In cases where the ashes are to be sent by rail or through the post, specially constructed containers shall be provided for this purpose, suitably labelled.

11. All mechanical apparatus used in the Crematorium shall be regularly overhauled and cleaned to ensure its being kept in perfect working order, and to prevent friction noises which are calculated to distract or disturb the mourners. Special attention should be paid to mechanical devices which are particularly prone to develop imperfections.

12. The greatest care should be taken in the appointment of members of the Crematorium staff, any one of whom may, by conduct or demeanour, detract from the atmosphere of reverence which is it endeavoured to create. In addition, it should be realized that the wrong type of man is capable of comment outside the Crematorium calculated to bring the Crematorium and Cremation into disrepute.

FOR FURTHER READING

AUTTON, N.
The Pastoral Care of the Bereaved. S.P.C.K. 1967

AUTTON, N.
The Pastoral Care of the Dying. S.P.C.K. 1966

BRANDON, S. G. F.
The Judgement of the Dead. Weidenfeld & Nicolson 1967

CAPLAN, G.
Principles of Preventive Psychiatry. Tavistock Publns. 1964

GORER, G.
Death, Grief, and Mourning in Contemporary Britain. Hutchinson 1963

HINTON, J.
Dying. Penguin 1967

LINDLEY, K.
Of Graves and Epitaphs. Hutchinson 1965

JONES, B.
Design for Death. Deutsch 1967

JUNG, C.
Memories, Dreams, Reflections. Collins 1963

MITFORD, J.
The American Way of Death. Hutchinson 1963

PATERNOSTER, M.
Thou Art There Also: God, Death, and Hell. S.P.C.K. 1967

TOYNBEE, A. (ED.)
Man's Concern with Death. Hodder & Stoughton 1968

WAUGH, E.
The Loved One. Chapman & Hall 1948